IN THE KITCHEN WITH KRIS

IN THE KITCHEN WITH KRIS

A KOLLECTION OF KARDASHIAN-JENNER FAMILY FAVORITES

KRIS JENNER

GALLERY BOOKS   **KAREN HUNTER PUBLISHING**

NEW YORK   LONDON   TORONTO   SYDNEY   NEW DELHI

Gallery Books
A Division of Simon & Schuster, Inc.
1230 Avenue of the Americas
New York, NY 10020

Karen Hunter Publishing,
A Division of Suitt-Hunter Enterprises, LLC
P.O. Box 632
South Orange, NJ 07079

First Karen Hunter Publishing/Gallery Books trade paperback edition March 2019

GALLERY and colophon are registered trademarks of Simon & Schuster, Inc.

For information about special discounts for bulk purchases,
please contact Simon & Schuster Special Sales at 1-866-506-1949
or business@simonandschuster.com.

The Simon & Schuster Speakers Bureau can bring authors to your live event.
For more information or to book an event contact the
Simon & Schuster Speakers Bureau at 1-866-248-3049
or visit our website at www.simonspeakers.com.

Designed by Ruth Lee-Mui

Manufactured in the United States of America

1   3   5   7   9   10   8   6   4   2

Library of Congress Cataloging-in-Publication Data

Jenner, Kris, 1955–
In the kitchen with Kris : a kollection of Kardashian-Jenner family favorites /
by Kris Jenner with Laura Randolph Lancaster.
pages   cm
1. Cooking.   I. Lancaster, Laura Randolph.   II. Title.
TX714.J46 2014
641.5—dc23
2014014073

ISBN 978-1-4767-2888-9
ISBN 978-1-4767-2889-6 (pbk)
ISBN 978-1-4767-2890-2 (ebook)

To the loves of my life: Kourtney, Kimberly, Khloé, Robert, Kendall, Kylie,
and to my beautiful grandchildren: Mason, Penelope, and North (and to all
my future little love bugs). I wrote this cookbook so you may pass our family's
favorite recipes on for generations to come. You are my heart and the reason
I love to cook. It is my life's biggest blessing to be your mom and your Lovey.

CONTENTS

Introduction   1

1. HAUTE TABLE

Setting the Table and the Tone   5

2. KRIS'S BASICS

Robert Kardashian's Cream of Wheat   14

Clarified Butter   15

3. APPETIZERS AND DIPS

Nicole's Chicken Nachos   19

Bruschetta with Tomato and Basil Topping   22

Baked Brie with Apricot Preserves   24

CiCi's Cheese Borags   27

Pâté Maîson   31

Green Olive Tapenade   33

Beef Sliders with Aïoli   35

Kris's Spicy Tomato Salsa   38

Italian Green Salsa   39

Layered Guacamole   40

4. SOUPS AND SALADS

M.J.'s Black-Eyed Peas Soup   45

Roasted Butternut Squash Soup   47

Homemade Cream of Tomato Soup   49

Hearty Chicken Soup   51

Curried Pumpkin Soup   54

Grilled Shrimp Caesar Salad   55

Holiday Chopped Salad   58

Romaine Hearts with Thousand Island Dressing   61

Chicken Salad with Pineapple   63

Iceberg Wedges with Avocado Green Goddess Dressing   66

5. IN THE KITCHEN

My La Cornue   69

The Fridge   70

6. MAIN COURSES

Chicken Pot Pies   75

Bruce's Meatloaf and Mashies   79

Grilled Veal Chops with Rosemary Spice Rub   82

Khloé's Buttermilk Fried Chicken   84

Armenian Lamb Shish Kebabs   87

Seared Sesame Tuna with Wasabi Aïoli   89

Shepherd's Pie–Stuffed Potatoes   92

Turkey and Cheese Enchiladas   94

Roast Chicken with Truffle Butter   97

Black Bean and Roasted Corn Chicken Quesadillas   99

Rainbow Turkey and Bean Chili   101

Pan-Roasted Salmon with Asparagus and Green Olive Tapenade   103

Grilled Swordfish Steaks with Tomato Salsa   105

7. PASTA

Kris's Pasta Primavera   111

Kim's Super Cheesy Macaroni and Cheese   113

Fettuccine with Sausage and Peppers   115

Red-and-White Lasagna   118

Fusilli with Tomato Basil Sauce   121

Pappardelle with Spring Vegetables   124

Lisa's Famous Mostaccioli   126

Penne with Vodka Sauce   129

Rich and Simple Tomato Sauce   131

Wild Mushroom Risotto   133

Spaghetti with Herbed Meatballs   137

8. VEGETABLES AND SIDES

Sweet Potato Soufflé   141

Auntie Dorothy's Armenian String Beans   142

Roasted Brussels Sprouts   143

Truffled Cauliflower Mash   144

Nana's "Wedding" Rice Pilaf   147

Grilled Eggplant with Scallions and Garlic   149

Wild Mushroom Stuffing   152

Spicy Sweet Potato Steak Fries   155

Crème Spinach Pie   156

Cranberry Orange Relish with Maple Syrup and Grand Marnier   158

Herbed Garlic Bread   160

Quick Cheese Rolls   161

Herbed Sourdough Bread   162

9. DESSERTS AND BAKED GOODS

Lemon Chiffon Pie   165

Berry Crumble   168

Magic Cookie Bars   170

Brownies   173

Berry Cobbler   177

Kim's Pumpkin Bread   179

Joey's Pecan Pie   182

Boozy Butterscotch Puddings with Salted Caramel   185

Chocolate-Dipped Coconut Macaroons   188

Chocolate Chip Banana Bread   190

Acknowledgments   193

Index   195

IN THE KITCHEN WITH KRIS

INTRODUCTION

When I married Robert Kardashian, I was twenty-two years old, and one of the gifts we received as a wedding present was six weeks at a cooking school in Los Angeles. It turned out to be one of the absolute best gifts we would receive because it literally laid the foundation for what would become a crucial part of our family—food and cooking.

I don't remember the name of the school, but I would go there several times a week and they covered everything from appetizers to desserts. I learned how to cook things I had never even eaten before. And I loved every minute of it. I would come home and practice the recipes on Robert and my mom and our friends, and I noticed that people were really enjoying the food. I discovered, "Hey, I can *really* cook!"

I love Christmas so much! Especially Santa.

When I was growing up, my mom was a single mother raising two kids and she worked. Sometimes she didn't have time to make it home to cook for us so I would cook for my sister and myself. I might make a poached egg and some toast or open a can of spaghetti or something. I remember feeling very grown-up when I had to cook and I knew when I had a family that this would be a major part of my job as a mother and a wife.

These cooking lessons brought it all home. It gave me the foundation to do all of the things I had envisioned when I was young and would think about raising a family. I knew cooking would be a part of that experience.

One of the first things I learned was how to make brownies. I share that recipe in this book and it was Rob's favorite. I also learned how to make a chicken liver pâté, which has become one of my mom's favorite things to eat. And they taught me how to make pasta. This is one dish that I improvised on, making various types of pasta and experimenting with sauces.

But more than learning how to cook, cooking school sparked in me the desire to make a home—to try new things. It helped broaden my horizons and I was able to pass that along to my children and my grandchildren, and now you!

Today, cooking—or rather, preparing meals in my kitchen—is one of my favorite things to do. No matter how hectic our schedules, or how crazy our lives may be, we start our day in the kitchen and we end it in the kitchen with a meal and a bottle of wine. The kitchen is where we share our stories from our day, where we laugh, and where we heal.

Cooking and my kitchen has become the glue that has kept our family strong throughout the years. And the recipes I'm sharing are part of our family's history and tradition—some very old, some new.

Early cooking lesson for Kourtney and Kim.

I collect cookbooks. I have more than a hundred. Rocco DiSpirito or William-Sonoma cookbooks are my go-to cookbooks because the recipes are so easy and simple. But I have cookbooks from all over the world. I buy them whenever I travel. I have several from France (one of my favorite places in the world), and I picked one up in Vienna recently. But my best cookbook is the one I have housed in several notebooks. I have a notebook for every kind of recipe imaginable. I have a notebook just for chili, stews, and soups. I have a notebook just for Thanksgiving, which is my second favorite holiday. I rotate dishes from year to year, but of course, there are family favorites that always make it to the table.

I have a notebook of desserts for everything from a Fourth of July cake (I use blueberries for the stars and rows of strawberries for the stripes) to an Easter Bunny cake, which I do every year. I dye the coconut green for grass and use jelly beans for the eggs. It's delicious!

I have a special spot in my heart for desserts because that's how I got my children interested in cooking. When they were little, I would have them in the kitchen with me baking cookies and making cupcakes. There would be frosting and mix everywhere and, of course, fights over who got to lick the bowl. One Christmas I spent hours in the kitchen making a gingerbread house. I mean a real gingerbread house! It actually took me two days to put it all together. And all of the kids ended up sick with stomachaches from eating half of the candy they were supposed to be using to put on the house. But those are memories that they will have forever.

I also keep traditional family recipes, such as Nana Helen's Beeshee. Helen was Robert's mother and she would make beeshee (which is an Armenian pastry like a pancake) every holiday. As Nana grew older, I knew she would not have the energy to make them much longer because they were a lot of work. So Kourtney, Khloé, and now Kendall learned the recipe and they can all make them almost as well as Nana did. The last time she made them, I videotaped it so that we would always have that recipe in our family and they would know exactly how it was done.

It's much more than food. It's tradition. It's legacy. It's love.

1. HAUTE TABLE

SETTING THE TABLE
AND THE TONE

One of the things I enjoy most about entertaining and cooking for my family is the joy I get from the table setting. You'd be surprised how very little effort can make a big difference in creating an amazing dining experience. Cooking for someone is such an expression of love, and so is the presentation. I know my family gets extremely excited when we celebrate a huge occasion or just get together for our Sunday dinners because they know how much love and energy I put into making it beautiful for them. I also love going to other people's homes for dinner because I always get entertaining inspiration and creative ideas from my friends.

Almost as important as the food is the table setting. I believe that cooking for someone is one of the best things you can do. It's a way of expressing how much you care about the people you love. I also believe that the table setting is an extension of that love. The amount of time you put into making sure things are beautiful, that your table makes a statement, or creates a mood, also says, "I love you!"

I am notorious for my table settings and my dishes. If I'm cooking an Italian meal, I will grab my red Hermès china to go with the red sauce (Fusilli with Tomato Basil Sauce, page 121).

I have five different kinds of Christmas dishes. I have nutcrackers, Santas, reindeer, and snowmen. If you can think of anything Christmas-y that can go on a table, I have it and have used it over the years.

I collect china and dishes. My children all know how obsessed I am with table settings and I've received several sets of Hermès dishes from my daughters. Table settings. Napkins and napkin rings. Baccarat crystal glasses and vases. Candles and candle holders. I'm obsessed with it all.

When I got married, nesting and creating this visual ambiance was so important to me. I somehow understood that it would be important to tying my family all together.

And over the years, it has. My children—and our family and extended family and friends—have come to expect a certain look and feel when they come over to share a meal. It's never "simple" or "normal."

For Rob's most recent birthday, I had a St. Patrick's Day theme because it fell on St. Paddy's Day. I had the table decorated with shamrocks and gold coins and green beads. It was over-the-top and tasteful at the same time. And he absolutely enjoyed it. Kim's birthday always falls around Halloween. When she was little, I would have a Halloween theme with pumpkin baskets, candy, and a pumpkin-themed cake. I would go the whole nine yards. (Some of my favorite pumpkin recipes in this book are inspired by Kim and her birthday.)

For holidays I go all out. I will set the table for Thanksgiving four days in advance. It takes me that long to get it just right, layering the different decorations, adding and taking things away until I can stand back and say, "Yes, that's it."

Some people paint, others make music and dance, I make table settings. That's my way of expressing my artistic and creative side.

And I love to see the smiles on the faces of my children and guests when they see what I've done. The key is to have fun with it. As long as it's done in the spirit of love, you are sure to make it beautiful.

Robert Kardashian, Papa, and Nana, the way I remember them, with my sweet baby boy, Rob.

2. KRIS'S BASICS

COMFORT FOOD

When Robert was diagnosed with esophageal cancer, it was already stage IV. The treatments made him so sick he would sometimes go for days without wanting anything to eat. Anything, that is, except Cream of Wheat. But he wouldn't eat just any Cream of Wheat. He wanted Cream of Wheat cooked by Kim.

"I'm thankful for all of my girls," Robert used to say. "Especially Kimberly." (I know he wasn't supposed to say that out loud, but he did.)

And Kim loved making Cream of Wheat for her father almost as much as he loved her cooking it for him. It was their special thing. Every bit as precious as the moments they spent together at the kitchen table sharing plans, stories, and dreams when Kim moved in with Robert after graduating high school.

The thing with the Cream of Wheat started when Robert became too ill to sit and eat with Kim at the kitchen table. So she would take the kitchen table to him. Whenever she could talk her father into eating (and let's face it, Kim can talk an Eskimo into

Kim and her dad.

buying ice cubes), she carried two bowls to her father's bedside—one empty and one filled with the Cream of Wheat she'd cooked for him in the kitchen. As Robert watched, Kim would sprinkle sugar into the empty bowl until the bottom was completely covered. Then she'd pour the Cream of Wheat on top, stirring the cereal into the sugar until the mixture was perfect. Not too thick. Not too thin. Just the way Robert liked it. To this day, neither Kim nor I can see a box of Cream of Wheat without remembering Robert, and how much we loved him.

When I heard the exciting news that my kids were pregnant, I fantasized about how much fun it was going to be to cook for my grandkids. I know Cream of Wheat will be one of their favorites!

ROBERT KARDASHIAN'S CREAM OF WHEAT

MAKES 2 SERVINGS

1 box Cream of Wheat

2 teaspoons sugar, or to taste

milk

1. Follow cooking instructions on box for two servings.

2. Evenly sprinkle the sugar on the bottom of a large shallow bowl until bottom is fully covered.

3. Slowly pour the Cream of Wheat over the sugar.

4. Stir until blended completely.

5. Add milk, to taste.

6. Serve warm—and with love.

CLARIFIED BUTTER

MAKES ABOUT 1½ CUPS

Butter has a wonderful taste, but, unfortunately, it doesn't make the best cooking fat because it burns more easily than oil. The culprits are the milk solids in the butter, which burn at a lower temperature than the fatty components. Clarified butter has the milk solids removed in a very simple technique so you can sauté or fry in the butter without it burning. In Armenia and other parts of the Mediterranean, butter is clarified to increase its shelf life, as the milk solids would sour before the fatty part. I use clarified butter in several of my recipes, including Nana's "Wedding" Rice Pilaf (page 147) and CiCi's Cheese Borags (page 27). But keep in mind that you can use it as you would any cooking oil to sauté meats or veggies.

1 pound (4 sticks) unsalted butter, cut into tablespoons

1. Melt the butter in a medium saucepan over medium heat until the butter is boiling. Reduce the heat to medium-low and let bubble for 2 minutes, make sure that the butter doesn't brown. Remove from the heat and let the butter stand for about 1 minute, or until cool.

2. Pour the butter into a glass measuring cup and let stand for about 5 minutes, or until the foam rises to the top. Skim off any foam. Pour the clarified butter into a jar or covered container, leaving behind any milky residue in the cup.

3. Refrigerate, uncovered, for at least 2 hours, until firm and chilled. Cover the jar and refrigerate.

Note: The clarified butter can be refrigerated for up to 3 months. Let the clarified butter come to room temperature before using.

3. APPETIZERS AND DIPS

NICOLE'S CHICKEN NACHOS

MAKES 8 TO 10 SERVINGS

This is the first dish I think of when I think of Nicole Brown Simpson. She was such an amazing cook. Everything she made was off-the-charts good. Her chicken nachos were so fabulous, they had a cult following. Back in the day, nobody in our circle would even think about throwing a party without serving Nicole's chicken nachos, that's how amazing they were. And for some reason they taste even more delicious when you are gathered around the living room watching sports with family and friends.

2 medium tomatoes, seeded, and cut into ½-inch dice

2 scallions, white and green parts, thinly sliced

¾ cup canned jalapeño slices, drained

Kosher salt

1½ cups (6 ounces) shredded sharp Cheddar cheese

1½ cups (6 ounces) shredded mozzarella cheese

One 8-ounce bag tortilla chips, preferably Have'a corn chips

1. Position a rack in the center of the oven and preheat the oven to 350°F.

2. In a medium bowl, mix together the tomatoes, scallions, and jalapeño slices and season with salt to taste. Set aside.

3. In another bowl mix together the Cheddar and mozzarella. Set aside.

4. On a large baking sheet or in a wide oven-safe casserole dish, spread half of the tortilla chips and sprinkle with half of the cheese mix. Bake until the cheese is just beginning to melt, about 5 minutes. Remove from the oven.

3 cups shredded cooked chicken breast

3 tablespoons chopped fresh cilantro, for garnish (optional)

One 3.8-ounce can sliced black olives

Kris's Spicy Tomato Salsa (page 38) or store-bought salsa

Sour cream

5. Sprinkle with half of the chicken and half of the tomato mixture. Top with the remaining tortilla chips. Sprinkle with the remaining chicken and the tomato mixture, and finish with the remaining cheese.

6. Return to the oven and bake until the top layer of cheese is completely melted, 15 to 20 minutes. Remove from the oven.

7. Garnish with the cilantro, if using, and black olives and serve immediately with the salsa and sour cream on the side.

Note: You could use 3 cups of Mexican cheese blend (Cheddar with other cheeses meant for Mexican cooking), but I like this blend of cheeses and I like to shred it fresh.

Me, Debbie Medina, and Linda Shulman in my favorite meeting place—
the kitchen—and there's Nicole feeding me one of her famous nachos.

BRUSCHETTA WITH TOMATO AND BASIL TOPPING

MAKES 8 SERVINGS

These are best served right off the grill. If you don't have a grill, simply toast the bread in the broiler. Use a flavorful extra-virgin olive oil because this is one time when you will taste the oil. Chopped tomatoes are the most popular topping, but this one has ricotta salata and other herbs along with the basil. You can use other toppings, such as the Green Olive Tapenade (page 33). You can also serve the toasted bread and toppings separately, and let your guests help themselves.

TOPPING

2 pounds ripe plum tomatoes, halved lengthwise, seeded, and cut into ½-inch dice

1 cup shredded ricotta salata cheese

½ cup finely chopped fresh basil

¼ cup finely chopped fresh flat-leaf parsley

¼ cup finely chopped fresh mint

¼ cup extra-virgin olive oil

1. To make the topping: In a medium bowl combine the tomatoes, ricotta salata, basil, parsley, mint, olive oil, garlic, lemon zest, lemon juice, and red pepper flakes. Season with salt and pepper to taste. Cover and let stand at room temperature for 1 to 3 hours to blend the flavors.

2. For the Bruschetta: Prepare an outdoor grill for direct cooking over medium-high heat. Brush the grill grate clean. For a charcoal grill, let the coals burn until covered with white ash and you can hold your hand just above the grill grates for 3 to 4 seconds. For a gas grill, preheat the grill on high, then adjust the heat to 450°F.

2 garlic cloves, minced

Finely grated zest of
1 lemon

2 tablespoons fresh
lemon juice

¼ teaspoon red pepper
flakes

Kosher salt and freshly
ground black pepper

BRUSCHETTA

8 wide slices crusty rustic
bread, cut ½ inch thick

¼ cup extra-virgin
olive oil

2 garlic cloves, peeled
but not crushed

3. Using a pastry brush, brush both sides of the bread with the olive oil. Place the bread on the grill. Cook, keeping the lid closed as much as possible, turning once, until both sides are seared with grill marks, about 1 minute per side. Rub the toasted slices with the garlic—the rough bread surface will grate the garlic onto the bread. Cut each bread slice in half crosswise and transfer to a napkin-lined basket to keep warm.

4. Drain the excess juices from the tomato topping. Top each bread half with a generous amount of the topping, transfer to plates, and serve.

BAKED BRIE WITH
APRICOT PRESERVES

MAKES 6 TO 8 SERVINGS

You can substitute other preserves for the apricots, if you wish. Raspberry is good, or even savory spreads like a tapenade. Serve as an appetizer, or even as dessert with fruit. Let the cheese cool a bit before serving so it isn't so runny.

One 13- to 16-ounce wheel Brie cheese, chilled

½ cup apricot preserves

2 tablespoons brandy

1 large egg

1 tablespoon whole milk

1 sheet frozen puff pastry, thawed, but still chilled

All-purpose flour, for dusting and rolling the pastry

Baguette slices, crackers, apple slices, or grapes, for serving

1. Position a rack in the center of the oven and preheat the oven to 400°F.

2. Using a sharp knife, trim and discard the top rind and halfway down on the sides, careful not to remove too much of the cheese. Set aside.

3. In a small bowl, whisk together the apricot preserves and brandy. Set aside.

4. In another small bowl, whisk together the egg and milk. Set aside.

5. Place the pastry sheet on a lightly floured work surface and dust the top with flour. Roll out the pastry to a 12-inch square.

6. Place the cheese on a large, rimmed baking sheet and spread the top with the preserves mixture.

7. Center the pastry over the cheese. Cut away the excess pastry leaving about a quarter-inch rim at the bottom. Reserve the trimmings. Tuck the pastry under the cheese to cover it.

8. Lightly brush the top and sides of the pastry with the egg mixture.

9. Using a small sharp knife or cookie cutter, cut the trimmings into decorations (such as leaves, strips, or rounds). Place the decorations on the pastry and lightly brush them with the egg mixture.

10. Bake until the pastry is golden brown, about 20 minutes. Do not overbake or the cheese may ooze out of the pastry.

11. Transfer to a serving platter and let cool for 10 minutes. Serve warm, with a knife. Cut into thin wedges and spread on baguette slices, crackers, apple slices, and grapes.

CICI'S CHEESE BORAGS

MAKES 56 BORAGS

If you look at my family tree, you'll find CiCi on the Kardashian side. (She is Robert's first cousin.) But if you studied our relationship, you'd see the two of us are as close as sisters. Through the ups and downs of my life, CiCi and I have stayed the best of friends. (It was CiCi who told American Airlines I was retiring when I couldn't work up the nerve to do it myself.)

CiCi is always cool under pressure, as I've learned many times over the course of our forty-year friendship. Her borags are a family tradition. They were always a hit at Nana Kardashian's barbecues (and my kids love them).

The folding part can be tricky at first, but it just takes a little practice. Give them a try. They're so worth the effort.

Serve as hors d'oeuvres. Some borags use just Jack cheese, but this recipe has three types of cheeses, including a ricotta salata (a firm, aged ricotta cheese) and three herbs for a truly great filling. Don't let the phyllo sheets scare you. Use a soft-bristle pastry brush to avoid tearing the phyllo; some cooks even use a brush fashioned from large feathers!

To avoid the thin pastry sheets from sticking together, thaw frozen phyllo dough overnight in the refrigerator. If thawed at room temperature, condensation can form, and the added moisture can make the sheets stick together.

FILLING

3 cups (about 14 ounces) shredded Monterey Jack cheese

1 cup (4 ounces) crumbled feta cheese

1 cup (4 ounces) shredded ricotta salata cheese

3 tablespoons finely chopped fresh dill

3 tablespoons finely chopped fresh mint

3 tablespoons finely chopped fresh flat-leaf parsley

2 large eggs, beaten

¼ teaspoon freshly ground black pepper

PASTRY

½ package (18 sheets) phyllo sheets, thawed overnight in the refrigerator

¾ cup melted butter

1. Position racks in the top third and center of the oven and preheat the oven to 350°F. Line two large rimmed baking sheets with parchment paper.

2. To make the filling: In a large bowl, combine the Monterey Jack, feta, ricotta salata, dill, mint, parsley, eggs, and pepper.

3. Unroll the phyllo sheets and stack on the work surface. Cover with a sheet of plastic wrap and a damp kitchen towel to keep the sheets from drying out.

4. Place a phyllo sheet, with the short side facing you, on the work surface. Using a soft pastry brush, gently brush the sheet with the melted butter.

5. Using a pizza wheel or a sharp knife, cut the phyllo sheet into thirds lengthwise.

6. Place a teaspoon of the filling on the bottom of one strip, about half inch from the bottom and slightly off center.

7. Starting at the right bottom corner of the strip, fold the phyllo strip over to cover the filling to meet the opposite long side of the strip. Lightly press down on the filled phyllo triangle to spread the filling.

8. Fold the phyllo triangle up, then over to the other side, continuing in a flag-folding fashion to form a filled triangle-shaped borag.

9. Transfer to a prepared baking sheet. Repeat with the remaining two phyllo strips.

10. Starting from step 4, continue with the remaining phyllo sheets, butter, and filling, placing the borags about a half inch apart on the baking sheets.

11. Brush the tops of the triangles with the remaining clarified butter and bake until the borags are golden brown and crisp, about 15 minutes.

Note: The borags can be stored at room temperature for up to 2 hours or covered loosely with plastic wrap and refrigerated for 1 day. Reheat in a preheated 350°F oven for about 10 minutes.

PÂTÉ MAÎSON

MAKES ABOUT 12 SERVINGS

This is my mom's favorite recipe. It's the second thing I learned to make when I took cooking lessons, right after Rob's favorite brownies. I fell in love with it all over again when I went to Paris recently and ordered it at this fabulous little bistro, and couldn't wait to get home to make it again.

This is the way I make it at home. And I think it's every bit as good as the pâté I had in Paris.

The mixture of nutmeg, cloves, cinnamon, and ginger is called quatre épices (four spices), and is a secret ingredient in many French pâté recipes. Don't be scared of flambéing the livers; just keep your wits about you and be safe. Pâté is always brown, so garnish with colorful fresh vegetables, fruits, and crackers.

I cup (2 sticks) unsalted butter, 10 tablespoons cold and cut into tablespoons

I Granny Smith apple, peeled, cored, and cut into ½-inch dice

I small yellow onion, finely chopped

I cup finely chopped shallots

1. Melt 3 tablespoons of the butter in a large skillet over medium heat. Add the apple and cook, stirring occasionally, until lightly browned, about 3 minutes, Add the onion, shallots, garlic, and bay leaf, and cook for about 4 minutes, or until the onion softens, stirring occasionally. Transfer the onion mixture to a large bowl. Set aside.

2. Add 3 tablespoons of the butter to the skillet and melt over medium-high heat. Add the chicken livers and cook for 5 to

2 garlic cloves, minced

1 bay leaf

One 16- to 20-ounce container chicken livers, drained and trimmed

1 teaspoon kosher salt

¼ teaspoon ground cinnamon

¼ teaspoon ground cloves

¼ teaspoon ground ginger

¼ teaspoon freshly grated nutmeg

¼ teaspoon freshly ground black pepper

Pinch of cayenne pepper

¼ cup Calvados or Applejack brandy

2 tablespoons heavy cream

1½ teaspoons fresh lemon juice

Finely chopped fresh flat-leaf parsley, for garnish

Finely chopped pistachios, for garnish

Baguette slices, crackers, or toast, for serving

7 minutes, turning them occasionally, until they are cooked through but slightly pink in the center. Sprinkle the livers with the salt, cinnamon, cloves, ginger, nutmeg, black and cayenne peppers and mix well. Reduce the heat to very low. Pour the Calvados into the skillet. Carefully ignite the Calvados (use either fireplace matches or a grill lighter) and let the flame burn until it extinguishes by itself. If the Calvados burns for longer than 30 seconds, cover the skillet with a lid to extinguish flames. Using a wooden spoon, scrape up any browned bits in the skillet. Add the liver mixture and its cooking liquid to the onion mixture. Let cool until tepid, about 30 minutes.

3. Remove the bay leaf from the onion mixture. Transfer the onion-and-liver mixture to a food processor. Add the heavy cream and lemon juice and pulse a few times to finely chop the livers. With the processor running, add the remaining cold butter, 1 tablespoon at a time, letting the livers absorb each addition before adding the next.

4. Line a 3½- to 4-cup terrine mold or small loaf pan with a large sheet of plastic wrap, letting the excess hang over the sides. Fill the mold with the pâté mixture and smooth the top. Cover with the overhanging plastic wrap, making sure that the top is completely covered. Refrigerate for at least 4 hours and up to 2 days, until chilled and firm.

5. Fold back the plastic wrap, invert the pâté onto a serving platter, and remove the mold and plastic wrap. Sprinkle the parsley and pistachios over the pâté as a garnish. Serve chilled, with the baguette slices, crackers, or toast.

GREEN OLIVE TAPENADE

MAKES ABOUT 1 1/2 CUPS

You can find bright green Castelnuovo olives at upscale delicatessens and grocery stores. They usually need to be pitted, which you can do with a cherry/olive pitter, or by smashing each olive under the flat, wide side of a knife and picking out the pit.

I like to serve this spread as a condiment to fish (Pan-Roasted Salmon with Asparagus and Green Olive Tapenade, page 103) and grilled meats, and it also makes a topnotch topping for bruschetta. When you think you don't have anything in the house to eat, cook up some thin pasta and toss it with this tapenade for a quick and simple meal.

1/4 cup pine nuts

1 garlic clove, peeled and smashed

1 cup pitted green Castelnuovo olives

1/3 cup plus 1 tablespoon extra-virgin olive oil

1/4 cup coarsely chopped fresh flat-leaf parsley

1/4 cup coarsely chopped fresh basil

1/4 cup coarsely chopped fresh mint

1. Heat a small cast-iron skillet over medium heat. Add the pine nuts and toast for 1 to 2 minutes, stirring often, until lightly toasted and fragrant. Transfer the pine nuts to a plate and let cool.

2. With the food processor running, add the garlic through the feed tube and mince. Stop the processor and add the pine nuts, olives, olive oil, parsley, basil, mint, thyme, capers, and lemon zest. Season with salt and pepper to taste. Pulse the machine until the mixture is almost a purée.

1 teaspoon finely chopped
fresh thyme

2 tablespoons nonpareil
capers, drained and rinsed

Finely grated zest of
1 lemon

Kosher salt and freshly
ground black pepper

3. Transfer to a container, cover tightly, and let stand for at least 1 hour to blend the flavors.

Note: The tapenade can be stored in the refrigerator for up to 3 days.

BEEF SLIDERS WITH AÏOLI

MAKES 12 SLIDERS

These mini burgers are so delicious that they never last at a gathering. The secret of a good burger is in the ground meat—use ground round, which has a fat content of about 15 percent. Mini dinner rolls make great slider buns, but if you can't find them, cut hot dog buns crosswise into three pieces. Enlist a second pair of hands to help you build the sliders before serving, and have the toppings ready and work assembly-line fashion.

AÏOLI

⅓ cup mayonnaise

1 large garlic clove, crushed through a press

1¼ teaspoons kosher salt

½ teaspoon freshly ground black pepper

SLIDERS

1 pound ground round (85% lean)

Olive oil, for brushing

8 thin 2-inch-square (about 3 ounces) slices sharp Cheddar cheese

1. To make the aïoli: In a small bowl, combine the mayonnaise and garlic. Cover and refrigerate for at least 1 hour to blend the flavors.

2. In a small bowl combine the salt and pepper.

3. In a medium bowl, mix half of the salt-and-pepper mixture with the ground round and divide into twelve 2-inch-wide patties. Brush the patties on both sides with the olive oil, place on a platter, and sprinkle with the remaining salt-and-pepper mixture. Let the patties stand at room temperature while preparing the grill.

12 miniature hamburger buns or dinner rolls

2 plum tomatoes, cut crosswise into 12 slices

12 slices dill or sweet pickle

½ cup baby arugula

4. Prepare a grill for direct and indirect cooking over high heat. Brush the grill grate clean. For a charcoal grill, let the coals burn until they are covered with white ash. Spread most of the coals on one side of the grill, scattering a few coals on the opposite side. For a gas grill, preheat the grill on high, and then turn one burner to very low.

5. Meanwhile, place the patties over the heated side of the grill. With the grill covered, grill the patties until the undersides are browned, about 2 minutes. Flip the patties and top each with a Cheddar slice.

6. Place the buns, cut sides down, on the unheated side of the grill. Cover and grill until the patties are browned, about 1 minute for medium rare sliders, and the buns are heated, taking care that the buns do not burn. Transfer the buns to a platter, and top each with a patty.

7. Spread each bun with some aïoli, then top with a tomato slice, a pickle slice, and a few arugula leaves. Close the bun and serve immediately.

KRIS'S SPICY TOMATO SALSA

MAKES ABOUT 2¾ CUPS

I love this salsa because it's as figure-friendly as it is fabulous. Especially when you think outside the tortilla chip bag.

It takes grilled salmon and chicken breast to a whole new level, too. When served with veggies, it's a dieter's dream. The tomatoes contain fiber and water, which helps you stay fuller longer. And they're loaded with lycopene, which helps build strong bones. But that's not even the best news about the lycopene: It helps protect your skin from the aging rays of the sun! I learned this last little tidbit while watching *How to Live to 100* on the Cooking Channel.

2 large beefsteak tomatoes, peeled, seeded, and cut into ¼-inch dice (2 cups)

½ medium sweet onion, such as Maui or Vidalia, finely diced (⅔ cup)

½ cup finely chopped fresh cilantro

¼ cup fresh lime juice

1 tablespoon red pepper flakes

1 tablespoon red pepper sauce, such as Tabasco

Kosher salt

In a medium bowl, combine the tomatoes, onion, cilantro, lime juice, red pepper flakes, and red pepper sauce. Season with salt to taste. Cover and let stand at room temperature for 30 minutes to blend the flavors. The salsa can be made up to 4 hours ahead. Drain excess liquid before serving. Serve at room temperature.

ITALIAN GREEN SALSA

MAKES ABOUT 1 1/4 CUPS

This Italian green salsa (salsa means sauce in Italian as well as in Spanish) is a wonderful way to perk up simple food that hasn't been seasoned with a lot of spices. Try it on grilled or baked fish or even a steak.

2 garlic cloves, peeled and crushed

1/2 cup packed fresh flat-leaf parsley

1/2 cup packed fresh basil

1/2 cup packed fresh mint

1/4 cup fresh lemon juice

2 tablespoons nonpareil capers, drained and rinsed

2 teaspoons anchovy paste, or 4 drained anchovy fillets packed in oil

3/4 cup extra-virgin olive oil

Kosher salt and freshly ground black pepper

1. With the food processor running, add the garlic through the feed tube and mince. Stop the processor and add the parsley, basil, mint, lemon juice, capers, and anchovy paste. Pulse the machine until the mixture is almost a purée. With the machine running, gradually drizzle in the olive oil through the feed tube. Season with the salt and pepper to taste.

2. Transfer to a container, cover tightly, and let stand for at least 1 hour to blend the flavors.

Note: The salsa can be stored in the refrigerator for up to 3 days.

LAYERED GUACAMOLE

Make this dish ahead for big parties. I usually make it with eight avocados because it goes so fast, and it's good to have leftovers. Serve with tortilla chips, of course, but it's also good with raw veggies.

GUACAMOLE

8 ripe avocados, pitted and peeled

One 8-ounce jar (1 cup) smooth salsa, such as Pace's Picante Sauce

1 teaspoon garlic salt

1 teaspoon onion powder

Seasoned salt and freshly ground black pepper

OTHER LAYERS

½ lemon wedge

1½ cups sour cream, stirred well to give it a smoother spreading consistency

1½ cups (6 ounces) sharp Cheddar cheese, grated

4 plum (Roma) tomatoes, seeded, cut into ½-inch dice, and patted with paper towels to remove excess moisture

8 scallions, white and green parts, finely chopped

One 3.8-ounce can sliced black olives, drained and dried

Tortilla chips

1. To make the guacamole: In a large bowl, using a potato masher, mash the avocados. Stir in the salsa, garlic salt, and onion powder. Season generously with the seasoned salt and pepper.

2. Level out the guacamole with a small rubber spatula, and squeeze lemon on top. Spread the sour cream evenly over the guacamole, then add a layer of grated cheese. Sprinkle the olives in a band around the perimeter of the guacamole, then a band of the tomatoes, and finish with the scallions to create a bulls-eye effect. The dip can be covered with plastic wrap and refrigerated for up to 4 hours.

3. Serve chilled, with the tortilla chips for dipping.

4. SOUPS AND SALADS

M.J.'S BLACK-EYED PEAS SOUP

MAKES 8 SERVINGS

It's a Southern thing. Eating black-eyed peas on New Year's Day, that is. My mother, Mary Jo, was born in Arkansas, and in the Jenner house, her recipe for this Southern classic has reached legendary status.

Just like it doesn't feel like Christmas until somebody puts up the tree, my mom has always said it just doesn't feel like New Year's until somebody cooks a pot of black-eyed peas.

If you weren't born or raised in the South, you may not know the black-eyed peas back story: According to Southern folklore, if you eat black-eyed peas on New Year's Day, you'll have a prosperous new year. And who doesn't love prosperity? It's just one of those things a girl needs if she plans to live independently, an important life lesson my mom passed down to me.

On a random note: It's also supposed to be bad luck to do laundry on New Year's Day. Whether you believe in such things or not, I say why tempt fate? Especially when you can avoid all possibility of bad karma by doing something way more fun than laundry, like hanging out in the kitchen with your kids making M.J.'s black-eyed peas.

Notes: The beans are soaked by the quick-soak method. If you prefer, put the beans in a bowl, cover completely with cold water, and let stand overnight at room temperature; drain and rinse.

This makes a brothy soup. If you like thick bean soup, blend half of the soup (without the ham) in a blender in batches, and return it to the pot.

1 pound dried black-eyed peas, picked over for stones

2 tablespoons regular olive oil

1 large yellow onion, cut into ½-inch dice

1 large leek (1 cup), white and pale green parts only, cut into ½-inch dice

1 large carrot, cut into ½-inch dice

1 large celery rib, cut into ½-inch dice

6 garlic cloves, minced

2 pounds ham hocks, sawed crosswise into a few pieces by the butcher

10 cups reduced-sodium chicken broth

2 bay leaves

1 teaspoon kosher salt, plus more to taste

½ teaspoon freshly ground black pepper, plus more to taste

1½ teaspoons finely chopped fresh thyme or ¾ teaspoon dried

1½ teaspoons ground cumin

½ teaspoon red pepper flakes

Chopped fresh flat-leaf parsley, for garnish

1. Rinse and drain the black-eyed peas in a colander. Transfer the black-eyed peas to a large saucepan and add enough water to cover by 2 inches. Bring to a boil over high heat. Boil for 2 minutes. Remove from the heat, cover, and let stand for 1 hour. Drain and rinse again.

2. Heat the olive oil in a soup pot over medium heat. Add the onion, leek, carrot, celery, and garlic, and cook, stirring occasionally, until the onion is translucent but not caramelized, about 5 minutes.

3. Add the black-eyed peas and stir well. Add the ham hocks, chicken broth, and bay leaves and bring to a boil over high heat, skimming off any foam that rises to the surface. Season the soup with the 1 teaspoon salt and ½ teaspoon pepper. Reduce the heat to medium-low and simmer, stirring occasionally, until the peas are very tender and the ham hocks are very tender when pierced with a meat fork, about 2 hours.

4. Remove the ham hocks, set aside, and let stand until cool enough to handle. When cooled, discard the skin, fat, and bones, and coarsely chop the meat. Return the meat to the soup and stir well. Season with salt and pepper to taste. Remove and discard the bay leaves. During the last few minutes of cooking, stir in the thyme, cumin, and red pepper flakes.

5. Ladle the soup into bowls, top each serving with a sprinkling of parsley, and serve hot.

ROASTED BUTTERNUT SQUASH SOUP

MAKES 4 TO 6 SERVINGS

Roasting the squash first brings out the sweet notes in the soup. The blend of thyme, ginger, nutmeg, and allspice, backed up with a hint of maple, makes this a terrific soup for a Thanksgiving dinner.

You can make it vegetarian by using a vegetable stock instead of chicken broth.

5 cups (20 ounces) butternut squash peeled, seeded, and cut into ½-inch dice

I tablespoon vegetable oil

½ teaspoon kosher salt, plus more to taste

¼ teaspoon freshly ground black pepper, plus more to taste

3 tablespoons unsalted butter

4 large shallots (1 cup), chopped

3 garlic cloves, finely chopped

½ teaspoon chopped fresh thyme

1. Position a rack in the center of the oven and preheat the oven to 400°F.

2. Toss the butternut squash and vegetable oil together on a large rimmed baking sheet and spread in an even layer. Season with the ½ teaspoon salt and ¼ teaspoon pepper. Place the squash in the oven and roast for about 30 minutes, or until lightly brown and tender, turning the squash occasionally with a metal spatula. Remove from the oven. Set aside.

3. Melt the butter in a large saucepan over medium heat. Add the shallots and garlic and cook, stirring occasionally, until softened, about 3 minutes. Add the squash, thyme, ginger, and allspice and stir well. Add the broth and bring to a simmer over high heat. Reduce the heat to medium-low

1 teaspoon peeled and finely grated fresh ginger

¼ teaspoon ground allspice

1 quart reduced-sodium chicken broth

½ cup heavy cream

2 tablespoons maple syrup, preferably pure Grade B (see Note)

¼ teaspoon freshly grated nutmeg

Crème fraîche, for garnish

and partially cover the saucepan. Simmer for 15 minutes to blend the flavors. Remove from the heat and let cool slightly.

4. In a blender purée the soup in batches (or purée in the saucepan with an immersion blender). Return the soup to the saucepan and stir in the heavy cream, maple syrup, and nutmeg. Heat over low heat, stirring often, until very hot but not simmering. Season with salt and pepper to taste.

5. Ladle into bowls and top each serving with a dollop of crème fraîche.

Note: Grade B maple syrup has a stronger maple flavor than Grade A syrup, making it better for cooking. It is increasingly available at supermarkets and price clubs—Trader Joe's is a good source. You can use Grade A syrup. By the way, the grades have nothing to do with quality and are based on the color of the syrup. Grade B is darker and thicker, and harvested late in the season, giving it a deeper flavor than Grade A.

HOMEMADE CREAM OF TOMATO SOUP

MAKES 6 TO 8 SERVINGS

With just a few minutes of effort, you can have homemade tomato soup that will put the canned stuff to shame. You can, however, leave the cream out if you have an issue with milk.

Salsa on top is a nice modern touch, but the soup is great without salsa as a retro favorite.

Serve with crusty bread or even saltine crackers.

4 tablespoons (½ stick) unsalted butter

large yellow onion, chopped

1 medium carrot, chopped

1 medium celery rib, chopped

2 garlic cloves, thinly sliced

1 teaspoon finely chopped fresh thyme or ½ teaspoon dried

¼ teaspoon kosher salt, plus more to taste

1. Melt the butter in a large saucepan over medium heat. Add the onion, carrot, celery, garlic, and thyme. Sprinkle with the ¼ teaspoon salt and ¼ teaspoon pepper. Cook, stirring occasionally, until the onions are translucent but not caramelized, about 5 minutes.

2. Add the chicken stock, tomatoes, and bay leaf and bring to a boil over high heat. Reduce the heat to medium-low and simmer until slightly reduced, about 30 minutes.

3. Discard the bay leaf. In batches, purée the tomato mixture in a blender (or purée in the saucepan with an immersion blender). Return the soup to the saucepan and stir in the

¼ teaspoon freshly
ground black pepper,
plus more to taste

4 cups reduced-sodium
chicken broth

One 28-ounce can
imported Italian tomatoes
in juice, preferably
San Marzano, coarsely
chopped

1 bay leaf

½ cup heavy cream

Italian Green Salsa
(page 39), for garnish
(optional)

heavy cream. Heat over low heat, stirring often, until very hot but not simmering. Season with salt and pepper to taste.

4. Ladle the soup into bowls, topping each serving with Italian Green Salsa, if using.

HEARTY CHICKEN SOUP

MAKES 8 TO 10 SERVINGS

This chicken soup recipe is absolutely my favorite go-to comfort food. It's something that I love to make in the fall when the weather starts to get a little cooler here in Southern California. Kendall, Kylie, and Rob always request this soup when they are feeling sick. It's also one of Bruce's favorites. I serve it with some delicious, crunchy French bread. You will be addicted!

You can save time by making great homemade soup with rotisserie chicken—no messing with raw chicken. Mexican flavor is added with the chili powder and cumin. You can also granish with tortilla chips to make a Mexican tortilla soup. This recipe is inspired by Cristina Ferrare's recipe.

STOCK

Two medium rotisserie chickens

1 medium yellow onion, quartered

1 medium carrot, coarsely chopped

1 medium celery rib, coarsely chopped

1. To make the stock: Remove the meat from the chickens. Shred and chop the meat into bite-size pieces, cover, and refrigerate to add to the soup later.

2. In a large pot, combine the chicken skin and carcass with 6 cups of water, the onion, carrot, and celery. Cook for 1 hour over medium heat, skimming off any foam that rises to the surface. Strain the stock through a colander into a large bowl, discarding the solids. Season to taste with salt and pepper.

SOUP

2 medium carrots,
cut into ½-inch dice

2 medium celery ribs,
cut into ½-inch dice

3 large scallions,
white and green parts,
thinly sliced

2 cups bite-size broccoli
or cauliflower florets,
or a combination

1 medium zucchini,
cut into ½-inch dice

1 medium squash, cut into
½-inch dice

1 teaspoon chili powder

1 teaspoon cumin

1 teaspoon Spike
seasoning, or another
brand of all-purpose
seasoning salt

¼ cup pearled barley

1 cup pastina pasta

3. To make the soup: Place the stock back into the large pot. Add the chicken, carrots, celery, scallions, broccoli or cauliflower, zucchini, squash, chili powder, cumin, Spike seasoning, and barley. Simmer for 1 hour.

4. Add the pastina pasta and cook for an additional 10 minutes.

Note: If soup is too thick, add water.

CURRIED PUMPKIN SOUP

MAKES 8 TO 10 SERVINGS

3 tablespoons unsalted butter

1 large white onion, thinly sliced

8 scallions, white and pale green parts only, thinly sliced (¾ cup)

1 tablespoon curry powder

½ teaspoon sugar

¼ teaspoon freshly grated nutmeg

One 29-ounce can of solid-pack pumpkin

4 cups reduced-sodium chicken broth

4 sprigs fresh flat-leaf parsley

1 bay leaf

2 cups heavy cream

Salt and freshly ground black pepper

1. Melt the butter in a large saucepan over medium heat. Add the onion and cook, stirring occasionally, until golden, about 5 minutes. Stir in the scallions and cook until they wilt, about 2 minutes. Stir in the curry powder, sugar, and nutmeg. Add the pumpkin and mix well.

2. Stir in the broth. Add the parsley and bay leaf and bring to a simmer. Reduce the heat to medium low and simmer, stirring occasionally, until slightly thickened, about 30 minutes. Remove the bay leaf.

3. In batches, purée the pumpkin mixture in a blender (or purée in the saucepan with an immersion blender). Return the soup to the saucepan, stir in the cream, and heat over low heat, stirring often, until very hot but not simmering. Season to taste with the salt and pepper. Ladle into bowls and serve hot.

GRILLED SHRIMP CAESAR SALAD

MAKES 4 TO 6 SERVINGS

Serve as a big salad for lunch or dinner, especially when the weather is hot.

This is an authentic Caesar dressing made with a coddled (barely cooked) egg. Use a pasteurized egg to avoid the "raw egg" issue of possible unhealthy bacteria. Or, try the mayonnaise-based dressing variation. Yes, you can leave out the anchovies, but the secret of a good Caesar is that you don't really notice them.

Caesar salad should always have croutons, but I like thick toasted bread—similar to that used in bruschetta—to provide the crunch. Allow one slice per person, but you may want to serve more on the side because they are slightly addictive.

Shrimp are labeled by count. For example, large shrimp are labeled 21–25 because that's how many are in a pound. For grilling, I prefer the very large ones that are under 15 shrimp to a pound (labeled U-15). These are big enough that they won't fall through the grill's grate, but a perforated grill topper is a good idea as an extra precaution. Or thread the shrimp onto metal skewers so they can be turned easily.

I allow 4 to 5 shrimp per person. Usually, an odd number of pieces look best on the plate.

DRESSING

1 large egg, preferably pasteurized

2 garlic cloves, peeled and crushed

2 tablespoons fresh lemon juice

1. To make the dressing: In a medium saucepan bring 2 inches of water to a boil. Using a slotted spoon, carefully add the egg (it should be covered with the water) and reduce the heat to medium-low. Cook for 1 minute at a brisk simmer. Remove the egg from the saucepan and transfer to a bowl of iced water. Let cool for about 3 minutes, or until easy to handle.

1 tablespoon Dijon mustard

1 tablespoon Worcestershire sauce

1 teaspoon red pepper sauce, such as Tabasco

1 teaspoon anchovy paste, or 2 drained anchovy fillets in oil, chopped

½ cup regular olive oil

¼ cup freshly grated Parmesan cheese

Kosher salt and freshly ground black pepper

SHRIMP

Finely grated zest of 1 lemon

2 tablespoons fresh lemon juice

2 tablespoons extra-virgin olive oil

1 garlic clove, minced

½ teaspoon red pepper flakes

¼ teaspoon kosher salt

¼ teaspoon freshly ground black pepper

16 to 20 (U-15 count) shrimp, peeled and deveined

2. Break the egg into a blender or mini food processor, scraping out any clinging white from the shell with a teaspoon. Add the garlic, lemon juice, mustard, Worcestershire sauce, red pepper sauce, and anchovy paste. Blend until the garlic is minced. With the machine running, slowly drizzle in the olive oil through the hole in the blender lid (or the feed tube of the processor) until the dressing is thickened. Add the grated Parmesan cheese and pulse to combine. Season with salt and pepper to taste. The dressing is very full-flavored, so you may not need much seasoning.

3. To prepare the shrimp: In a medium bowl, whisk together the lemon zest, lemon juice, olive oil, garlic, red pepper flakes, salt, and pepper. Add the shrimp and toss to coat. Cover the bowl and refrigerate, stirring occasionally, for at least 30 minutes and up to 1 hour.

4. To prepare the bread: Brush the bread on both sides with the olive oil.

5. Prepare an outdoor grill for direct cooking over medium-high heat. Brush the grill grate clean. For a charcoal grill, let the coals burn down until they are covered with white ash, and you can hold your hand about an inch above the grate for 3 or 4 seconds. For a gas grill, preheat on high, then adjust the heat to medium-high (450° to 500°F).

6. Add the bread slices to the grill and cook with the lid closed as much as possible, occasionally flipping the bread, until toasted, about 2 minutes. Remove the bread from the grill. Set aside.

4 to 6 slices crusty
French or Italian bread,
cut ½-inch thick

Extra-virgin olive oil

SALAD

2 heads romaine hearts,
bottoms trimmed, leaves
separated

One chunk (4 ounces)
Parmesan cheese

7. Place a perforated grill topper on the grate, if using, and let it heat for a few minutes. Drain the shrimp and place them on the grill. Cook about 5 minutes, with the lid closed, until the shrimp are opaque and firm, turning once halfway through cooking. Remove the shrimp from the grill. Set aside.

8. In a very large bowl, toss the lettuce with about half of the dressing. Arrange the toasted bread around the edge of a large platter. Heap the lettuce over the bread and top with the shrimp. Using a vegetable peeler, shave as many Parmesan cheese curls over the salad as you like. Serve immediately.

MAYONNAISE CAESAR SALAD DRESSING

Substitute ¾ cup mayonnaise for the egg and olive oil. Put the mayonnaise in a medium bowl and whisk in the remaining ingredients.

HOLIDAY CHOPPED SALAD

MAKES 12 TO 16 SERVINGS

This is a reliable salad for winter holiday parties because it doesn't depend on tomatoes and other summer vegetables to be tasty. Have everything prepared and refrigerated well ahead of time, then toss just before serving.

VINAIGRETTE

¼ cup Champagne or white wine vinegar

3 tablespoons minced shallots

1 tablespoon Dijon mustard

2 teaspoons finely chopped fresh tarragon

1 teaspoon finely chopped fresh thyme

1 teaspoon finely chopped fresh flat-leaf parsley

1 cup extra-virgin olive oil

Kosher salt and freshly ground black pepper

SALAD

One 5- to 7-ounce bag mesclun salad greens

One 14-ounce can hearts of palm, drained, rinsed, and cut into ½-inch-thick rounds

2 ripe pears, cored and thinly sliced

½ head radicchio, cored and coarsely chopped

½ head fennel, cored and cut crosswise into thin slices

2 heads Belgian endive, cored and coarsely chopped

2 carrots, cut into thin strips

1 small red onion, cut into thin half-moons

7 ounces enoki mushrooms, roots trimmed and cut into small clusters

1 cup coarsely chopped glazed pecans

1 cup crumbled blue cheese

½ cup pomegranate seeds

½ cup dried currants

1. To make the vinaigrette: In a small bowl, whisk together the Champagne vinegar, shallots, mustard, tarragon, thyme, and parsley. Gradually whisk in the olive oil. Season with salt and pepper to taste.

2. In a very big serving bowl, toss together the salad greens, hearts of palm, pears, radicchio, fennel, Belgian endive, carrots, onion, and mushrooms. Add the vinaigrette and toss. Add the pecans, blue cheese, pomegranate seeds, and currants and toss again. Serve immediately.

Note: The dressing can be covered and refrigerated for 3 days. Whisk again before using.

ROMAINE HEARTS WITH THOUSAND ISLAND DRESSING

MAKES 4 SERVINGS

Too often, Thousand Island dressing is a sweet, gloopy mess. This homemade version returns it to its original glory, with tangy bits of pickle, mildly spicy chili sauce, and just a little sweet relish.

Thick and rich, it should be served on firm, crisp lettuce, such as romaine or iceberg, as it will wilt delicate salad greens.

THOUSAND ISLAND DRESSING

Makes 1½ cups

1 large egg

¾ cup mayonnaise

⅓ cup plus 1 tablespoon ketchup-style chili sauce

4 drained cornichons (small sour pickles), finely chopped, or 2 tablespoons finely chopped dill pickles

1½ tablespoons minced yellow onion

1 tablespoon capers, drained and rinsed

1. Bring a small saucepan of water to a boil over high heat. Carefully add the egg to the water. Remove the saucepan from the heat and cover. Let stand for 15 minutes. Transfer the egg to a bowl of ice water and let stand for about 10 minutes, until the egg is chilled. Peel the egg and finely chop.

2. In a medium bowl, combine the mayonnaise, ⅓ cup ketchup-style chili sauce, half of the chopped egg, cornichons, onion, capers, sweet relish, lemon juice, and garlic. Season with salt and pepper to taste. Cover and refrigerate for at least 1 hour to blend the flavors.

1 tablespoon sweet relish

1 teaspoon fresh
lemon juice

1 small garlic clove,
minced

Kosher salt and freshly
ground black pepper

SALAD

3 romaine hearts,
separated into individual
leaves

3. Divide the romaine hearts among four dinner plates, stacking the leaves, and top each stack with a generous amount of dressing. Sprinkle the remaining egg over each and serve.

CHICKEN SALAD WITH PINEAPPLE

MAKES 16 TO 20 SERVINGS

One of the best ways to entertain, especially at a big brunch or lunch, is with a big chicken salad, loaded with good sweet and crunchy ingredients. My version has a creamy curry dressing—you can add more curry powder for a spicier flavor. This salad can be made a day ahead, and just needs a few minutes (or seconds) of attention when it comes time for serving. You can substitute 3 cups of chunked rotisserie chicken for the freshly cooked chicken, if you wish.

CHICKEN

3 pounds boneless, skinless chicken breast halves

Kosher salt

DRESSING

1 cup high-quality mayonnaise, such as Best Foods or Hellman's

¼ cup sour cream

½ teaspoon curry powder, or more to taste

1. To prepare the chicken: Place the chicken in a shallow saucepan or deep-sided skillet with enough water to cover chicken and a pinch of salt, and simmer until the chicken is completely cooked through. Let cool and cut into cubes.

2. To make the dressing: Whisk the mayonnaise, sour cream, and curry powder together in a small bowl. Cover and refrigerate until ready to use.

3. To make the salad: Toss the chicken, celery, pineapple tidbits, water chestnuts, almonds, chutney, lemon juice,

SALAD

2 cups chopped celery, about 6 large celery ribs

Two 20-ounce cans pineapple tidbits, drained well

One 8-ounce can sliced water chestnuts, drained well

1 cup whole roasted almonds, such as Blue Diamond almonds

½ cup mango chutney, such as Major Grey's

⅓ cup plus 1 tablespoon fresh lemon juice

¼ cup dried currants or seedless raisins

Kosher salt

1 head bronze lettuce, leaves separated, washed, and patted dry with paper towels

Sweet paprika, for garnish

and currants together in a large bowl. Mix in the dressing. Season to taste with the salt.

4. Arrange the lettuce leaves on a large platter. Heap the salad on the lettuce and sprinkle with paprika. Serve chilled.

ICEBERG WEDGES WITH AVOCADO GREEN GODDESS DRESSING

Green Goddess dressing has been around for a long time, but this version is different from most, thanks to the avocado and hints of basil and mint which gives it extra flavor and color. How did the dressing get its name? In the 1920s, the play *The Green Goddess* played San Francisco, and it was such a hit that the Palace Hotel made this dressing to honor the show.

This is also fantastic as a dip with raw veggies or even cooked shrimp.

Note: I like to serve this salad for special occasions.

DRESSING
Makes 2 cups

1 ripe avocado, pitted, peeled, and cubed

½ cup sour cream

¼ cup packed fresh parsley leaves

2 tablespoons coarsely chopped fresh tarragon

1 tablespoon coarsely chopped fresh basil

1 tablespoon coarsely chopped fresh mint

3 tablespoons fresh lemon juice

3 tablespoons minced shallot

2 teaspoons anchovy paste

1 garlic clove, peeled and crushed

½ cup regular olive oil

Kosher salt and freshly ground black pepper

SALAD

1½ heads iceberg lettuce, cored and cut into 6 equal-size wedges

Here are all my goddesses and one goddess-to-be.

1. To make the dressing: In a food processor or a blender, purée the avocado, sour cream, parsley, tarragon, basil, mint, lemon juice, shallot, anchovy paste, and garlic.

2. Gradually add the olive oil through the feed tube and process until smooth. Season with salt and pepper to taste. Transfer to a bowl, cover, and refrigerate for at least 1 hour to blend the flavors. The dressing can be made up to 1 day ahead.

3. Place an iceberg wedge onto each of 6 dinner plates and top each wedge with a generous amount of the dressing. Serve chilled.

5. IN THE KITCHEN

MY LA CORNUE

A few years ago, I was at Jennifer Lopez's house, and while taking the grand tour of her beautiful home, I got stuck in the kitchen. I was literally awestruck. I had fallen completely in love.

J-Lo had this stove that I had never seen before. It wasn't just a stove, it was a piece of art. It was the Holy Grail of stoves. It was, I found out, a La Cornue. Before seeing hers, I bought stoves for function—making sure it had enough burners, that the oven heated evenly, and things like that. Of course, I thought my stoves were nice. But I had no idea that a stove could be the centerpiece of a kitchen in a way that turned that kitchen into a masterpiece.

I had a great time at Jennifer's house, but I couldn't stop thinking about her stove. The next week, I bought a La Cornue stove. One problem—once it was installed the rest of my kitchen looked drab. So I called my designer and told him that I wanted to renovate my kitchen. Not just a little spruce-up, but a total and complete makeover, and I wanted the design to center around the La Cornue stove that I had just bought.

I know it sounds crazy but I never thought I would be so happy with my kitchen as I am now. That La Cornue is the best piece of furniture in my entire house. For some reason, it makes me believe that I can cook better. I know it's silly. But it does.

I don't know if the food tastes better, but I know I sure have a lot more fun cooking on it.

THE FRIDGE

My refrigerator has a personality of its own. (It probably needs its own Instagram account, too.) It is definitely a conversation piece when people come to my home. It's not the refrigerator, per se, but how I organize it.

I started doing it this way when I got married at twenty-two, and started a family. It became a thing to make my home as special as possible. It started with making sure that my children had their special drinks lined up in such a way that they could just go in the fridge and grab their drink. But I have now taken that to a whole new level.

All of my children have definitely borrowed my refrigerator organizing. It has become a family competition to see who has the most organized refrigerator. (Khloé may have won this one.) It really is very funny.

Today, even though many of my kids have moved out and are on their own, I still like to make sure that I keep things I know all of my kids like. So I have a row of a certain kind of yogurt for Penelope, and a row of Mason's special juice . . . even North has her favorites! I make sure to have the favorite drink of every one of my kids in my fridge at all times. Can you guess which drinks are the favorite of which of my children by looking at the picture of my refrigerator?

6. MAIN COURSES

CHICKEN POT PIES

MAKES 6 INDIVIDUAL POT PIES

Make these in classy, individual servings for a really special dinner party. This is one of the best pot pies you will ever eat.

PASTRY DOUGH

2 cups all-purpose flour, plus more for dusting

1 teaspoon dried tarragon (optional)

½ teaspoon salt

¼ teaspoon freshly ground black pepper

14 tablespoons (1¾ sticks) cold unsalted butter, cut into ½-inch cubes

⅓ cup ice water, as needed

FILLING

Four 6-ounce chicken breasts, boneless and skinless

½ teaspoon kosher salt, plus more to taste

Special Equipment: Six 2-cup ramekins or onion soup bowls.

1. To make the pastry dough: In a medium bowl whisk together the flour, tarragon if using, salt, and pepper. Cut the butter into the flour mixture with a pastry blender or two knives until crumbly with some pea-size pieces of butter. Gradually stir in the ice water, 1 teaspoon at a time, until the dough starts to clump. (When you press a handful of the mixture, it should stick together, so add more water as needed.) Form the dough into a thick disk and wrap in plastic wrap. Refrigerate for at least 1 hour and up to 2 until chilled. The dough can be refrigerated for 1 day. When ready to use, let stand at room temperature for about 10 minutes to soften slightly. If the dough is too cold, it will crack when rolled out.

2. Preheat the oven to 350°F.

¼ teaspoon freshly ground black pepper, plus more to taste

1½ cups heavy cream

2 small carrots, halved lengthwise and cut into ½-inch-thick slices

½ small fennel bulb, cored, thinly sliced

1 small zucchini, quartered lengthwise, and cut into ½-inch-thick slices

6 asparagus stalks, woody stems discarded, cut into ¼-inch-long pieces

1 cup frozen black-eyed peas or green peas, thawed

½ cup (1 stick) unsalted butter

1 leek (white and pale green parts only), well rinsed and thinly sliced

3 tablespoons minced shallot

2 garlic cloves, minced

⅓ cup plus 1 tablespoon all-purpose flour

1½ cups reduced-sodium chicken broth, heated to steaming

¼ cup Cognac or brandy

1 tablespoon finely chopped fresh tarragon

1 large egg yolk beaten with 1 tablespoon milk, for glaze

3. To make the filling: Place the chicken breasts in a shallow baking dish just large enough to hold them in a single layer. Season the chicken with the ½ teaspoon salt and ¼ teaspoon pepper. Pour the heavy cream over the chicken and cover with aluminum foil and bake for 25 to 30 minutes, until the chicken feels firm when pressed with a fingertip. Turn off the oven. Transfer the chicken to a chopping board and let cool for 5 minutes. Reserve the cream. Cut into bite-size pieces (the chicken may not be completely cooked) and transfer to a bowl. Cover and refrigerate.

4. Bring a large saucepan of salted water to a boil over high heat. Add the carrots, fennel, zucchini, asparagus, and black-eyed peas and blanch for about 2 minutes until they turn a shade brighter and are crisp and tender. Drain in a colander, rinse under cold running water, and drain again. Add the vegetables to the bowl with the chicken and refrigerate.

5. Melt the butter in a medium saucepan over medium heat. Add the leek, shallot, and garlic and cook 4 to 5 minutes, stirring often, until the leeks are tender and translucent—but not caramelized. Sprinkle in the ⅓ cup flour and stir well. Reduce the heat to medium-low and cook for about 1 minute, stirring constantly. You do not want the flour to brown. Stir in the hot broth, Cognac, and the reserved cream and bring to a simmer over medium heat, whisking often. Return the heat to medium-low and, whisking occasionally, simmer for about 5 minutes, or until the sauce is reduced to the consistency of thick heavy cream. Stir in the

tarragon and season with salt and pepper to taste. Pour into a large heatproof bowl and let cool until tepid. Cover and refrigerate for at least 1 hour until chilled. (Or you can pour the sauce into the heatproof bowl and place the bowl in a roasting pan half-filled with ice water. Let stand, stirring often, until the sauce is cold, about 30 minutes.)

6. Preheat the oven to 350°F.

7. Stir the chicken and vegetables together with the sauce. Divide the chicken filling evenly among the ramekins or onion soup bowls.

8. Divide the chilled dough into sixths and shape each into a 3-inch diameter disk. For each pot pie, on a lightly floured work surface, roll out one pastry disk into an $\frac{1}{8}$-inch-thick round about 2 inches wider than the diameter of the ramekin. Lightly brush the pastry disk with the egg yolk glaze. Place the pastry, glazed side down, over the top of the ramekin, pressing it into the sides of the dish so that the pastry is taut, like the top of a drum.

9. Place in the refrigerator for 10 to 30 minutes.

10. Place the filled ramekins on a large rimmed baking sheet. Brush the tops with the remaining glaze and pierce a slit in the top of each with the tip of a small sharp knife. Bake until the tops are golden brown and a dinner knife inserted through the slit in the pastry for about 5 seconds comes out coated with the hot liquid, about 45 minutes. Serve hot.

They say the way to a man's heart is through his stomach. This was certainly true with Bruce.

BRUCE'S MEATLOAF AND MASHIES

MAKES 4 TO 6 SERVINGS

Meatloaf and Mashies is one of my favorite comfort food meals to make and it's also very sentimental to me. I met Bruce Jenner on a blind date set up by our friends Candace and Steve Garvey. We went to the Ivy at the Shore in Santa Monica, and Bruce ordered Meatloaf and Mashies. I will never forget how much he enjoyed that meal. It became one of my favorite things to cook because he loved it so much.

Note: I will sometimes add a layer of thinly sliced mozzarella cheese and thinly sliced bell peppers on the top 15 minutes before it is done baking to make it even more yummy and beautiful.

BRUCE'S FAVORITE MEATLOAF

2 pounds lean ground beef

½ cup carrots, finely diced

¼ cup celery, finely diced

1 large onion, finely diced

1 teaspoon minced garlic

½ cup sundried tomatoes, chopped

½ cup Parmesan, grated

½ cup packaged bread crumbs

⅔ cup diced canned tomatoes

2 eggs

1 teaspoon kosher salt

1 teaspoon white pepper

One 8-ounce package sliced mozzarella cheese, optional

⅓ cup ketchup (for the top)

BRUCE'S FAVORITE MASHIES

2 pounds unpeeled Russet potatoes

½ cup half and half

¼ cup (½ stick) salted butter

Kosher salt

1. Sauté vegetables with garlic until onions are translucent and let cool. Add remaining ingredients to sautéed vegetables. Mix together. Mold into a large buttered loaf pan. Cover the loaf with a thin layer of ketchup (and mozzarella, if using) and bake at 350°F until firm to the touch. The internal temperature should be 140°F. Let cool slightly before slicing.

2. Place potatoes in large pot and cover with cold water. Bring to boil, reduce heat to a simmer, and cook until very tender (about 20–30 minutes). Drain potatoes and return to pot. Add half and half and butter, and beat with a handheld electric mixer until smooth. Add salt to taste, and beat to incorporate.

GRILLED VEAL CHOPS WITH ROSEMARY SPICE RUB

MAKES 4 SERVINGS

Veal chops have a neutral taste that lets them pick up flavors from marinades and rubs. They should be cooked to medium to develop extra flavor from browning. But because they are lean, take care not to overcook them, which can dry them out. The solution is to grill them to medium, and then let the chops continue cooking a bit from the retained heat.

You can also cook these indoors in a grill pan. Brown the chops for 5 minutes per side, then roast the chops in a 450°F oven for about another 5 minutes.

CHOPS

4 bone-in veal rib chops (10 ounces each), cut 1-inch thick

3 garlic cloves, cut into 24 slivers

2 tablespoons extra-virgin olive oil

ROSEMARY SPICE RUB

1 tablespoon kosher salt

Grated zest of 1 lemon

1. Using the tip of a small sharp knife, poke 6 slits into each veal chop, and insert a garlic sliver into each slit. Brush the veal chops with the olive oil.

2. To make the rub: In a small bowl, mix together the salt, lemon zest, rosemary, black pepper, and paprika. Sprinkle evenly over both sides of the veal chops and using your fingers, rub the spice mixture into the chops.

3. Place the chops on a plate, cover with plastic wrap, and refrigerate for at least 2 hours and up to 8. Remove from the

2 teaspoons finely
chopped fresh rosemary

1 teaspoon freshly ground
black pepper

½ teaspoon sweet
paprika

refrigerator and let stand at room temperature for 30 minutes before grilling.

4. Prepare an outdoor grill for direct cooking over high heat. Brush the grill grate clean. For a charcoal grill, build a fire and let it burn until covered with white ash. Mound the coals on one side of the grill, leaving the other side empty. For a gas grill, preheat on high, then turn one burner off.

5. Place the chops on the hot area of the grill (over the coals or the ignited burner). Grill, with the lid closed, and without moving or flipping the chops, until the undersides are well browned, about 4 minutes. Flip the chops and continue grilling with the lid closed, until the other sides are browned, about 4 minutes more. Move the chops to the cooler area of the grill (the empty side of the charcoal grill or the turned-off burner of the gas grill). Continue grilling, with the lid closed, until the meaty part of a chop feels somewhat firm when pressed with a finger, 3 to 5 minutes more. If you want to use an instant-read thermometer to check the chops' temperature, insert the probe horizontally through the side of the chop into the center. The temperature should read 145°F.

6. Transfer the chops to a platter and let stand for 5 minutes. Serve hot.

KHLOÉ'S BUTTERMILK
FRIED CHICKEN

MAKES 4 SERVINGS

By the time Khloé was twelve I could call her if I had invited a bunch of people over and was running late and ask her to "handle it" until I got home. She wouldn't miss a beat. Khloé would whip up a chicken dish, make a big salad, set the table, get some fresh-cut flowers from the garden for the table, and have it all ready before the first guest (or I) arrived.

While all of my kids can cook something, Khloé is the one who really took after me in the kitchen—right down to how she sets her table, the china she uses, and what kind of candles she gets. And while she has mastered most of my recipes, she has certainly created quite a few of her own.

But I *really* knew Khloé was the best cook in the family the first time I tasted her fried chicken. Some dishes you can fake your way through. (Soups, salads, and salsas come to mind.) But only really good cooks can make really good fried chicken.

I learned from years of watching Khloé how to make perfect fried chicken every time.

Note: Use a small chicken—large ones don't cook through by the time the crust is browned. Do not drain the fried chicken on paper towels; the crust will get soggy.

One 3½ pound chicken, cut into 2 drumsticks, 2 thighs, 2 wings, and 2 breast halves

2 cups buttermilk

1 tablespoon kosher salt

1½ teaspoons sweet paprika

1½ teaspoons freshly ground black pepper

1 teaspoon garlic powder

1 teaspoon onion powder

½ teaspoon cayenne pepper

1 cup all-purpose flour

Vegetable shortening

1. Combine the chicken pieces and the buttermilk in a 1-gallon plastic storage bag and refrigerate for at least 8 hours and up to 12.

2. Drain the chicken in a colander. In a small bowl, mix together the salt, paprika, black pepper, garlic powder, onion powder, and cayenne. Sprinkle over the chicken, tossing to coat the chicken evenly. Put the flour in a paper bag. One at a time, shake the chicken in the flour to coat (shaking off the excess flour), and then place on a large baking sheet. Let the chicken stand for about 15 minutes to help set the coating.

3. Over high heat, melt enough shortening in a large 12-inch-deep skillet, preferably cast iron, to come halfway up the side of the skillet and heat until a deep-fat (candy) thermometer reads 360°F. Add the drumsticks, thighs, and wings to the skillet (they should bubble immediately in the oil). Cook over high heat, adjusting the heat as needed so that the oil bubbles steadily and maintains a temperature of around 325°F, turning the chicken occasionally, until the chicken is a deep golden brown and an instant-read thermometer inserted in the thickest part of the thigh reads 170°F, 12 to 15 minutes. Using tongs, transfer the chicken to a wire cake rack set over a rimmed baking sheet to drain.

4. Return the oil temperature to 360°F. Repeat with the chicken breast halves. Serve the chicken within a couple of hours of cooking. Do not refrigerate.

ARMENIAN LAMB SHISH KEBABS

MAKES 4 SERVINGS

When my kids were growing up, every other weekend in the summer we would all come together at Nana's (Robert's mom's) house for a big family cookout. Everyone would bring a dish. But there were staples. Of course, Nana's "Wedding" Rice Pilaf (page 147) would always be part of the menu. And these lamb kebabs were also a big hit. Uncle Jack was the one known for manning the grill. For the longest time, these were known as Uncle Jack's Shish Kebabs. But they soon became a family favorite that we all cook.

Note: The Armenian marinade for lamb kebabs is thick with tomato paste and seasoned with unusual spices. If you've never tried this kind of marinade before, you are in for a treat. It's really good served with grilled pita bread.

MARINADE

1 medium yellow onion, finely chopped

One 6-ounce can tomato paste

½ cup extra-virgin olive oil

2 tablespoons red wine vinegar

1. To make the marinade: In a large stainless steel or glass bowl, combine the onion, tomato paste, olive oil, vinegar, allspice, red pepper flakes, black pepper, and bay leaves.

2. Add the lamb and mix well to coat. Cover and refrigerate for at least 6 or up to 24 hours.

3. Prepare an outdoor grill for direct cooking over high heat. Brush the grill grate clean. For a charcoal grill, let the coals

2 teaspoons ground allspice

2 teaspoons red pepper flakes

½ teaspoon freshly ground black pepper

3 large bay leaves

LAMB KEBABS

3½ pounds leg of lamb, boneless, well-trimmed, and cut into 16 pieces about 1½- to 2-inch cubes

2 small red onions, each cut into 6 wedges

1 large green bell pepper, cored, seeded, and cut into 12 pieces

Olive oil

2 teaspoons kosher salt

burn until covered with white ash and you can hold your hand 1 inch above the cooking grate for about 2 seconds. For a gas grill, preheat on high, then adjust the temperature to 500°F.

4. Remove the meat from the marinade. For each kebab, thread 4 lamb pieces, 2 red onion wedges, and 2 green bell pepper pieces onto long metal skewers, alternating the meat and vegetables as desired, but not packing them too closely together. Let the kebabs stand at room temperature for 15 to 20 minutes to lose their chill. Brush the kebabs all over with the oil and season with the salt to taste.

5. Cook the kebabs, with the lid closed as much as possible, turning the kebabs occasionally, until the meat is seared on all sides and the vegetables are crisp and tender, 10 minutes for medium rare. To check the meat for doneness, cut into a lamb piece down to the skewer. The lamb is too small to check with a meat thermometer.

6. When done let stand for 3 minutes. Serve hot.

SEARED SESAME TUNA
WITH WASABI AÏOLI

MAKES 4 SERVINGS

Sushi fans love this dish. Buy the best tuna you can, preferably sushi grade. Go to a good fish market so they can cut for the thickness you need. Tuna is best served very rare because it dries out if cooked too long.

You can easily turn this into a main course salad. Make a little extra marinade, and toss it with a bag of baby arugula with grape tomatoes and a sliced sweet onion. Spread the salad on a platter, top with the tuna, and drizzle with some of the aïoli, serving the remaining aïoli on the side.

AÏOLI

⅓ cup mayonnaise

1 tablespoon wasabi paste (or 1 tablespoon wasabi powder mixed with 1 tablespoon water)

1 garlic clove, crushed through a press

MARINADE

¼ cup sake

¼ cup reduced-sodium soy sauce

1. To make the aïoli: In a small bowl, mix together the mayonnaise, wasabi paste, and garlic. Cover and refrigerate.

2. To make the marinade: In a small bowl, whisk together the sake, soy sauce, rice vinegar, sesame oil, cilantro, ginger, and garlic.

3. Reserve 2 tablespoons of the marinade. Pour the remaining marinade into a glass or ceramic pie plate. Add the tuna, cover with plastic wrap, and refrigerate for 30 minutes, turning the tuna after 15 minutes.

¼ cup rice vinegar (not seasoned)

2 tablespoons toasted sesame oil

2 tablespoons finely chopped fresh cilantro

2 teaspoons peeled and finely grated fresh ginger

2 garlic cloves, minced

TUNA

Two 12-ounce, 1½-inch-thick, center-cut tuna loin steaks, preferably sushi-grade ahi

1 teaspoon freshly ground black pepper

½ teaspoon kosher salt

⅓ cup sesame seeds

1 tablespoon peanut oil or grape seed oil

1 cup micro greens or baby arugula

1 scallion, white and green parts, very thinly sliced, for garnish

4. Remove the tuna from the marinade and pat dry with paper towels. Season both sides of the tuna with the pepper and salt.

5. Spread the sesame seeds on a plate and evenly coat the tuna on both sides with the sesame seeds. Transfer to a clean plate.

6. Put the aïoli in a small plastic storage bag. Using scissors, snip off a bottom corner tip of the bag to make a small opening. You now have a temporary "pastry bag." Squeeze the aïoli into the corner of the bag near the snipped opening.

7. Heat the peanut oil in a large nonstick skillet over high heat until the oil is very hot but not smoking. Add the tuna and cook until the sesame seeds on the underside are toasted, about 2 minutes. Turn the tuna and cook the other side, about 2 minutes more. Transfer to a carving board and let stand for 2 minutes. The tuna will be very rare. Using a thin, sharp knife, cut the tuna across the grain into ¼-inch-thick slices.

8. For each serving, place a quarter of the greens in the center of a dinner plate. Top with the seared tuna slice and drizzle with a teaspoon or two of the reserved marinade. Squeeze five dime-size pools of the aïoli, equally spaced, around the tuna and greens, in a circle on the plate. Sprinkle the sliced green onion over the tuna and serve.

SHEPHERD'S PIE–STUFFED POTATOES

MAKES 6 TO 8 SERVINGS

This is old-fashioned "Mom Cuisine" at its best. Be flexible with serving sizes, as some people will find one potato half to be sufficient, but big appetites may eat three halves. Shepherd's pie means different things to different cooks, but basically it is a meat filling (often beef, sometimes lamb, hence the shepherd in the name) with a mashed potato topping.

TOPPING

6 large baking potatoes, about 10 ounces each, scrubbed and pierced with a fork

½ cup (1 stick) unsalted butter, at room temperature

One 5.2-ounce package herb-and-garlic spread, such as Boursin

Kosher salt and freshly ground black pepper

1 large egg yolk

2 tablespoons finely chopped fresh chives

1. Preheat the oven to 400°F.

2. Place the potatoes on the oven rack and bake for 45 to 55 minutes, until tender when pierced with the tip of a small sharp knife.

3. Meanwhile, make the filling: In a large skillet over medium-high heat, cook the bacon, stirring occasionally, until the bacon is crisp and browned, about 8 minutes. Using a slotted spoon, transfer the bacon to paper towels to drain. Pour off all but 2 tablespoons of the fat from the skillet.

4. Add the onion, carrot, celery, and garlic to the skillet and cook, stirring occasionally, until the onion is softened, about

4 strips bacon, cut into 1-inch pieces

1 large yellow onion, chopped

1 medium carrot, coarsely shredded

1 medium celery rib, cut into ¼-inch dice

2–3 cloves garlic, minced

1 pound (85% lean) ground round

3 tablespoons tomato paste

1 tablespoon Worcestershire sauce

1 tablespoon finely chopped fresh thyme

1 cup hearty red wine

½ cup reduced-sodium beef or chicken broth

1 cup thawed frozen peas

Kosher salt and freshly ground black pepper

Vegetable oil for baking dish

3 minutes. Add the ground round and raise the heat to medium-high. Cook, stirring occasionally and breaking up the meat with the side of the spoon, until the meat begins to brown, about 6 minutes. Pour off any excess fat from the skillet. Return to medium heat and stir in the tomato paste, Worcestershire sauce, and thyme. Stir in the wine and bring to a boil, scraping up any browned bits in the skillet. Stir in the beef broth, 1 cup water, and the reserved bacon. Bring to a simmer and reduce the heat to medium-low. Simmer, stirring occasionally, until the cooking juices have reduced and the meat mixture is thick, about 40 minutes. Stir in the peas and remove from the heat. Season with salt and pepper.

5. When the potatoes are tender, remove them from the oven and let stand until just cool enough to handle. Cut each warm potato in half lengthwise. Using a spoon, scoop out the flesh from each potato half into a medium bowl, leaving a ¼-inch thick shell. Using a handheld electric mixer or potato masher, mash the potatoes with the butter and cheese spread. Season with salt and pepper to taste. Beat in the egg yolk and chives.

6. Lightly oil a large baking dish that will hold the potato halves in a single layer. Fill the potato halves with equal amounts of the filling. Place the potatoes in the dish. Spoon the mashed potatoes on top of the filling.

7. Transfer to the oven and reduce the oven temperature to 375°F. Bake until the potato topping is tinged golden brown, about 20 minutes. Serve hot.

TURKEY AND CHEESE ENCHILADAS

MAKES 6 SERVINGS

I use leftover holiday turkey for this. You can also use roasted turkey breast from the delicatessen, the meat from a rotisserie chicken, or roast chicken leftovers. This is my go-to recipe after Thanksgiving.

Often you can only find mild enchilada sauce at the supermarket. To spice it up, add 1 chipotle chile from a can, chopped, or season it with chili powder.

2 tablespoons unsalted butter

I medium yellow onion, chopped

3 cups shredded and coarsely chopped cooked turkey

One 19-ounce can enchilada sauce

I cup (4 ounces) shredded sharp Cheddar cheese

I cup (4 ounces) shredded jalapeño Jack cheese

Six 6-inch (fajita-size) flour tortillas

1. Preheat the oven to 350°F.

2. Melt the butter in a skillet over medium heat. Add the onion and cook, stirring occasionally, until translucent, about 5 minutes. Transfer to a bowl and let cool slightly. Stir in the turkey, ¼ cup of the enchilada sauce, ½ cup of the Cheddar cheese, and ½ cup of the Jack cheese.

3. Spread a half cup of the enchilada sauce in the bottom of a 9 × 13-inch baking dish. Pour the remaining enchilada sauce into a pie plate. Place a tortilla in the sauce. Add a sixth (about ½ cup) of the filling to the center of the tortilla and roll up the enchilada. Place the rolled enchilada, seam side down, in the prepared dish. Repeat with the remaining

¾ cup sour cream, at
room temperature

Chopped fresh cilantro,
for garnish

tortillas and filling. Pour any remaining sauce in the pie plate over the enchiladas. Sprinkle with the remaining Cheddar and Jack cheeses.

4. Bake until the sauce is bubbling and the cheese is melted, about 20 minutes. Let stand for 5 minutes. Serve hot, adding a dollop of sour cream and a sprinkle of cilantro to each serving.

ROAST CHICKEN WITH TRUFFLE BUTTER

MAKES 6 SERVINGS

White truffle butter is a magic ingredient. When you find it (at upscale grocers and specialty stores), buy an extra package to keep in the freezer. You can get it through mail order, too.

One 5½-pound roasting chicken

1 bunch (about 30 sprigs) fresh thyme

One 3-ounce container white truffle butter, well softened

Extra-virgin olive oil

2 teaspoons kosher salt

1 teaspoon freshly ground black pepper

1 small yellow onion, cut into 8 wedges

1 small head garlic, unpeeled, cut in half crosswise

1 cup reduced-sodium chicken broth

1. Remove the chicken giblets and save for another use. Remove the yellow pads of fat in the tail area and discard. Rinse the chicken under cold running water and pat dry with paper towels.

2. Finely chop enough of the thyme leaves (discarding the stems) to make 2 teaspoons. Reserve any remaining thyme sprigs.

3. Slip your fingers underneath the chicken skin at the breast and separate the skin from the flesh. Do not bother with the wings and back, but do try to reach as much of the drumsticks and thighs as possible. Smear the softened truffle butter under the chicken skin. Massage the skin to distribute the butter as evenly as possible over the chicken flesh.

4. Brush the entire chicken with the olive oil and season, inside and out, with the salt and pepper. Stuff the body cavity with the onion, garlic, and reserved thyme sprigs. Tie the chicken legs together with kitchen string, and tuck the wing tips behind the shoulders. Sprinkle the outside of the chicken with the chopped thyme leaves. Place the chicken on a rack in a roasting pan and let stand for 30 minutes.

5. Position a rack in the center of the oven and preheat the oven to 425°F.

6. Roast the chicken until an instant-read thermometer inserted in the thickest part of the thigh without touching a bone reads 170°F, about 1½ hours. Tilt the chicken so the cavity juices run into the pan. Transfer to a carving board and let stand for 10 to 15 minutes.

7. Pour the pan drippings into a small glass bowl and let stand for 3 minutes. Skim off and discard any fat on the surface. Return the degreased juices to the pan. Cook on stovetop over medium-high heat until sizzling. Add the chicken broth and bring to a boil, scraping up the browned bits in the pan with a wooden spoon. Cook until the liquid reduces by half, about 3 minutes. Season with salt and pepper to taste. Pour into a small bowl.

8. Carve the chicken and serve drizzled with the pan sauce.

BLACK BEAN AND ROASTED CORN CHICKEN QUESADILLAS

MAKES 6 SERVINGS

It's fun to make Mexican food at home. Be sure that you are using good quality, fresh ingredients.

FILLING

1 tablespoon olive oil

1 medium yellow onion, chopped

1 jalapeño, seeded and minced

2 garlic cloves, minced

½ teaspoon ground cumin

½ teaspoon dried oregano

2 cups shredded cooked chicken, store-bought or leftovers

1½ cups (6 ounces) shredded Cheddar or Mexican cheese blend

½ cup crumbled fresh cojita or feta cheese (see Notes)

1. To make the filling: Heat the oil in a medium saucepan over medium heat. Add the onion, jalapeño, and garlic and cover. Cook, stirring occasionally, until the onion is translucent, about 5 minutes. Stir in the cumin and oregano and cook uncovered for 1 minute more. Transfer the onion mixture to a large bowl and let cool.

2. Meanwhile, prepare an outdoor grill for direct cooking over medium heat. Brush the grill grate clean. For a charcoal grill, let the coals burn down until they are covered with white ash and you can hold your hand about an inch above the cooking grate for about 3 seconds. For a gas grill, preheat on high, then adjust the heat to medium (400°F).

3. Add the chicken, Cheddar, cojita, black beans, corn kernels, and cilantro to the cooled onion mixture and mix well. For each quesadilla, spread a generous ½ cup of the chicken

One 15.5-ounce can
Cuban black beans,
drained well but not
rinsed (see Notes)

1 cup thawed frozen
fire-roasted corn kernels
(see Notes)

2 tablespoons finely
chopped cilantro

Twelve 8-inch flour
(soft taco) tortillas

Cooking oil spray

Diced avocado, diced
plum tomatoes, chopped
fresh cilantro, sour cream,
and red pepper sauce, for
serving.

Kris's Spicy Tomato Salsa
(page 38) and hot sauce,
for serving

mixture on a tortilla, leaving a ½-inch border. Top with a second tortilla to make a quesadilla "sandwich." Spray both sides of the quesadilla with cooking spray.

4. Grill the quesadillas, with the lid closed, until the undersides are toasted, about 3 minutes. Flip the quesadillas and grill until the other sides are toasted and the cheese is melting, about 3 minutes more.

5. Using a pizza wheel or large knife, cut each quesadilla into six to eight wedges. Serve hot, with the avocados, tomatoes, cilantro, sour cream, salsa, and red pepper sauce on the side.

Notes: Cojita is a Mexican cheese that is sold either fresh (when it is crumbly and similar to feta) or aged (also called añejo and hard enough to be grated, like Romano or Parmesan cheeses). This recipe uses fresh cojita.

Cuban black beans are cooked with onion, green pepper, garlic, vinegar, and spices. Trader Joe's has a proprietary brand. If necessary, substitute a 15-ounce can of Latino-style black bean soup, which usually has whole beans and is not puréed. For either product, the beans should be drained, but not rinsed.

Frozen roasted corn kernels are available at Trader Joe's and some natural food stores. To make your own, heat 1 tablespoon olive oil in a large nonstick skillet over medium-high heat. Add 1 cup thawed frozen corn kernels and cook, stirring occasionally to let the kernels take on some color, until browned, about 5 minutes.

RAINBOW TURKEY AND BEAN CHILI

MAKES 8 SERVINGS

This mild dish will please many palates. Adjust the spiciness to taste by adding more jalapeños, chipotle, or chili powder. Don't use the extra-lean (99% lean) white-meat-only ground turkey, or the meat will be too dry. Use standard (90 to 93% lean) ground turkey. Serve with your favorite toppings, such as shredded Cheddar and chopped onion or scallion. A rainbow of colorful beans gives the chili its name.

3 tablespoons regular olive oil

1 large red onion, chopped

1 large carrot, cut into ½-inch dice

1 medium red bell pepper, cored, seeded, and cut into ½-inch dice

1 medium yellow bell pepper, cored, seeded, and cut into ½-inch dice

1 jalapeño, seeded and finely chopped

4 garlic cloves, minced

2 tablespoons tomato paste

1. Heat the oil in a large saucepan over medium heat. Add the red onion and carrot and cook, stirring occasionally, until they begin to soften, about 3 minutes. Stir in the red and yellow pepper and the jalapeño and cook, stirring occasionally, until the onion is translucent, about 3 minutes more. Stir in the garlic and cook until softened, about 1 minute. Add the tomato paste, chipotle chili, cumin, chili powder, and paprika and stir well. Cook, stirring constantly, or until the spices are toasted and fragrant, about 1 minute.

2. Raise the heat to medium-high. Add the turkey and cook, stirring often and breaking up the meat with the side of a spoon, until the turkey becomes opaque, about 6 minutes. Stir in the tomatoes and their juices, the beer, and the bay

1 canned chipotle chile in adobo sauce, finely chopped, with 1 tablespoon adobo sauce

1 tablespoon ground cumin

2 teaspoons chili powder

1 teaspoon Spanish smoked sweet paprika (see Note)

1 1/3 pounds ground turkey (90 to 93% lean)

One 28-ounce can Italian plum tomatoes in their juice, preferably San Marzano, coarsely chopped, juices reserved

One 12-ounce bottle Mexican dark beer, such as Negra Modelo or Dos Equis

1 bay leaf

One 15-ounce can cannellini (white kidney) beans, drained and rinsed

One 15-ounce can black beans, drained and rinsed

2 cups reduced-sodium chicken broth

Kosher salt and freshly ground black pepper

Warm corn tortillas, diced avocado, sour cream, grated cojita cheese, and finely chopped fresh cilantro, for serving

leaf. Reduce the heat to medium-low and simmer, stirring often, for 10 minutes.

3. Stir in the cannellini and black beans and the chicken broth. Return the liquid to a boil over high heat, then reduce the heat to medium-low. Simmer, stirring often, until the liquid has reduced and thickened, about 1 hour.

4. Season with salt and pepper to taste. Discard the bay leaf. Spoon the chili into bowls and serve hot, with the tortillas, avocado, sour cream, cojita cheese, and cilantro on the side.

Note: Spanish smoked paprika, also called *Pimentón de la Vera*, is made from red peppers dried over oak coals. Look closely at the label to be sure that you are getting the mild sweet (*dulce*) version and not the spicy (*picante*) one.

PAN-ROASTED SALMON WITH ASPARAGUS AND GREEN OLIVE TAPENADE

MAKES 4 SERVINGS

This is a restaurant-worthy main course that you can prepare at home. Serve with couscous or quinoa.

Many markets now sell 6-ounce portions of center-cut salmon fillets. They are more expensive, but they ensure that everyone will get the same-size servings of the plump, desirable center section, and no one is left with the thin tail section.

The tangy goat cheese pairs well with the asparagus and the buttery salmon. But if you aren't a goat cheese fan, just top each fillet with a slice of unsalted butter.

1 pound asparagus, woody stems trimmed

Four 6-ounce center-cut salmon fillets, skin on

Olive oil

½ teaspoon kosher salt

¼ teaspoon freshly ground black pepper

Four ½-inch thick rounds rindless goat cheese, at room temperature

4 tablespoons crumbled goat cheese

1. Position a rack in the center of the oven and preheat the oven to 350°F.

2. Bring a large saucepan of salted water to a boil over high heat. Add the asparagus and cook until just crisp and tender, 2 to 4 minutes, depending on the thickness of the asparagus. Drain and rinse under cold running water to stop the cooking. Pat the asparagus dry with paper towels. Season with salt and pepper to taste.

Green Olive Tapenade
(page 33)

Lemon wedges,
for garnish

3. Heat a very large nonstick skillet over medium-high heat. Brush the salmon on both sides with the olive oil, then season the flesh side with ½ teaspoon salt and ¼ teaspoon pepper. Place the salmon in the skillet, flesh down, and cook until the flesh is seared, about 2 minutes. Turn the salmon over and cook until the skin is seared, about 2 minutes more. Scatter the seasoned asparagus over the salmon. Place the skillet in the oven and cook until the asparagus is reheated and the salmon is opaque with a slightly rosy center when pierced with the tip of a small sharp knife, 3 to 5 minutes more. If the asparagus is done before the salmon, transfer to a plate and tent with aluminum foil to keep warm.

4. Divide the asparagus among four dinner plates. Transfer a salmon fillet to each plate. Top each fillet with a goat cheese round. Sprinkle each fillet with 1 tablespoon of crumbled goat cheese. Add a heaping tablespoon of the tapenade next to each fillet. Serve immediately with the lemon wedges.

GRILLED SWORDFISH STEAKS WITH TOMATO SALSA

MAKES 4 SERVINGS

This dish has a fantastic thick and clinging marinade that also goes well with chicken and pork. Serve with Kris's Spicy Tomato Salsa (page 38), if you wish.

½ cup fresh lime juice

¼ cup low-sodium soy sauce

3 tablespoons Dijon mustard

2 tablespoons finely chopped fresh dill

2 garlic cloves, crushed through a press

1 teaspoon freshly ground black pepper

½ cup extra-virgin olive oil

Four 7-ounce swordfish steaks, each cut 1 inch thick

Kris's Spicy Tomato Salsa (page 38)

Lime wedges, for serving

1. To make the marinade: In a medium bowl, whisk together the lime juice, soy sauce, mustard, dill, garlic, and pepper. Gradually whisk in the olive oil.

2. Arrange the swordfish in a large baking dish large enough to hold them in a single layer. Pour the marinade over the swordfish and turn the fish to coat it on both sides. Cover the dish with plastic wrap and refrigerate, occasionally turning the fish over, for 1 to 2 hours.

3. Prepare an outdoor grill for direct cooking over high heat. Brush the grill grates clean. For a charcoal grill, let the coals burn until they are covered with white ash and you can hold your hand just above the cooking grate for 1 to 2 seconds. For a gas grill, preheat the grill on High.

4. Remove the swordfish from the marinade, shaking off any excess marinade. Put the swordfish on the grill. Cook, with the lid closed as much as possible, until the underside is seared with grill marks, 3 to 4 minutes. Flip the swordfish over and continue grilling, with the lid closed, until the swordfish is barely opaque when pierced in the center with the tip of a small sharp knife, 3 to 4 minutes more. Serve hot with the tomato salsa and lime wedges.

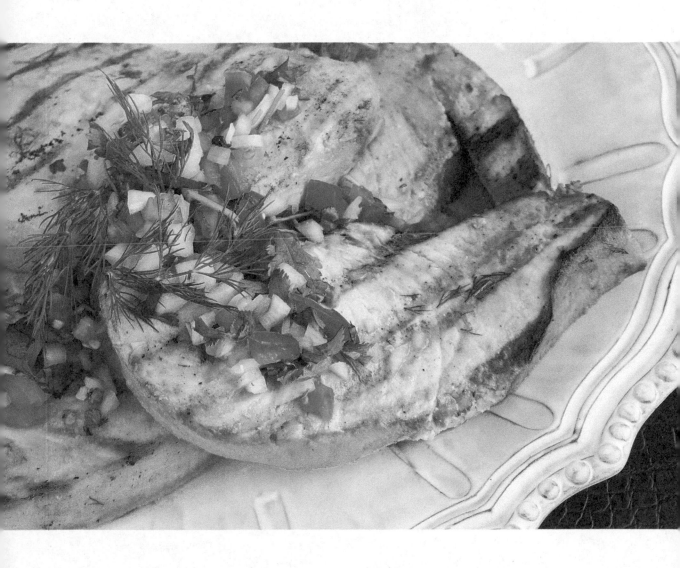

7. PASTA

KRIS'S PASTA PRIMAVERA

MAKES 4 TO 6 SERVINGS

I started making this dish shortly after I got married to Robert Kardashian. As a young couple, we had a lot of friends and we would often visit one another on the weekends or entertain at our house. Of course, food would be a big part of our gatherings. And you could never show up empty-handed.

I don't know who, but someone brought a pasta primavera to one of our get-togethers, and it was simple and delicious. I got the recipe and started making it not just when we visited friends, but for our family. It quickly became a Kardashian family favorite.

On Rob's last birthday, I asked him what he wanted and he said, "Just make me dinner. And make sure you make your pasta primavera . . . and your brownies." (He had a whole list of other dishes he wanted, too. And I made them all!)

Khloé has also borrowed this recipe and she swears hers is better. I disagree.

Note: I use lots of fresh vegetables, but no tomatoes. You can make this with just about any pasta. I prefer farfalle (bowties). Add a dollop of ricotta cheese, sautéed mushrooms, whatever. Just keep it vegetarian.

I pound farfalle (or your favorite pasta)

¼ cup extra-virgin olive oil

2 large carrots, cut into ½-inch dice

½ head broccoli, broken into small florets

I zucchini, halved lengthwise and cut into ¼-inch-thick half-moons

I red bell pepper, cored, seeded, and cut into ¼-inch-wide strips

I green bell pepper, cored, seeded, and cut into ¼-inch wide strips

I yellow bell pepper, cored, seeded, and cut into ¼-inch wide strips

I garlic clove, minced

Kosher salt and freshly ground black pepper

½ cup freshly grated Parmesan cheese, plus more for serving

¼ cup chopped fresh basil

1. Bring a large pot of salted water to a boil over high heat. Add the farfalle and cook according to the package directions until al dente.

2. Meanwhile, heat the oil in a large skillet over medium heat. Add the carrots and cover the skillet. Cook, stirring occasionally, until the carrots soften, about 5 minutes. Add the broccoli and zucchini and cook, uncovered, stirring occasionally, until they soften, about 3 minutes more. Add the red, green, and yellow peppers and cook, stirring often, until they are tender, about 5 minutes. During the last few minutes, stir in the garlic. Season with salt and pepper to taste. Remove from the heat and partially cover the skillet with its lid to keep the vegetables warm.

3. When the farfalle is done, scoop out and reserve ½ cup of the cooking water. Drain the farfalle well. Return the farfalle to its pot. Add the vegetables, Parmesan cheese, and basil. Mix well, adding enough of the reserved cooking water to melt the cheese into a light sauce. Season again with salt and pepper to taste. Serve hot, with more Parmesan cheese on the side.

KIM'S SUPER CHEESY MACARONI AND CHEESE

MAKES 6 SERVINGS

Lately, we've been having monthly dance parties at the Jenner House and you'll never guess who I ask to bring the mac and cheese—Kim. I don't know what she puts in it, but it's fabulous. So fabulous, in fact, I honestly believe it can hold its own against any mac and cheese recipes out there.

I developed my own recipe, inspired by Kim's recipe. I'm proud to say my family loves it as much as Kim's. And Khloé's Buttermilk Fried Chicken (page 84) is an amazing complement to this dish.

With six different types of cheese, this is a mac and cheese for people who really love the stuff and want a very special version to serve to friends and family.

If you don't have all six cheeses, you can make a really fantastic variation with 8 ounces Velveeta, 1 cup shredded sharp Cheddar, and 1 cup shredded Gruyère.

6 tablespoons (¾ stick) unsalted butter, plus softened butter for the baking dish

1 pound elbow macaroni

3 tablespoons all-purpose flour

1 tablespoon dry mustard powder

1. Preheat the oven to 350°F. Lightly butter a 9 × 13-inch baking dish.

2. Bring a large pot of salted water to a boil over high heat. Add the elbow macaroni and cook according to the package directions until al dente. Do not overcook the macaroni as it will soften when baked. Drain well.

3 cups whole milk, heated

½ yellow onion, shredded on the large holes of a box grater

½ teaspoon sweet paprika

1 bay leaf

8 ounces pasteurized processed cheese, such as Velveeta, cubed

1 cup (4 ounces) shredded sharp Cheddar cheese

¼ cup crumbled goat cheese

¼ cup shredded Gruyère cheese

¼ cup shredded mozzarella cheese

¼ cup freshly grated Parmesan cheese

Kosher salt and freshly ground black pepper

3 large eggs, beaten

1 cup panko bread crumbs

3. Meanwhile, melt 3 tablespoons of the butter in a large saucepan over medium heat. Whisk in the flour and the dry mustard. Reduce the heat to low and let cook, but do not brown, whisking often, for 2 minutes. Whisk in the hot milk, being sure the mixture is smooth. Whisk in the shredded onion, paprika, and bay leaf and bring to a simmer over medium heat, whisking often. Raise the heat to medium-low and simmer, whisking often, until the sauce is slightly reduced and the consistency of thick heavy cream, about 10 minutes. Remove from the heat.

4. Mix the Velveeta, Cheddar, goat cheese, Gruyère, mozzarella, and Parmesan together in a medium bowl. Add three-quarters of the cheese mixture to the sauce. Let stand for 1 minute, then stir until the cheeses melt. Season with salt and pepper to taste. Stir in the beaten eggs and mix well. Add the macaroni and mix well. Spread in the prepared baking dish and top with the remaining cheese mixture.

5. Melt the remaining 3 tablespoons butter in a medium skillet over medium heat. Add the panko and stir well. Sprinkle evenly over the macaroni mixture. Bake until the sauce is bubbling around the edges and the topping is golden brown, about 30 minutes. Let stand for 5 minutes. Serve hot.

FETTUCCINE WITH SAUSAGE AND PEPPERS

MAKES 4 TO 6 SERVINGS

Make the sauce while the pasta water is coming to a boil and the pasta cooks. This ensures the pasta and the sauce are done at about the same time. This is the kind of pasta that any Italian grandma would be happy to serve.

1 pound fettuccine or other long pasta

4 tablespoons extra-virgin olive oil

1 large red bell pepper, cored, seeded, and cut into ½-inch-wide strips

1 large yellow bell pepper, cored, seeded, and cut into ½-inch-wide strips

1 large green bell pepper, cored, seeded, and cut into ½-inch-wide strips

1 pound hot Italian sausage, casings removed

5 garlic cloves, minced

½ teaspoon red pepper flakes

1. Bring a large pot of salted water to a boil over high heat. Add the fettuccine and cook according to the package directions until al dente.

2. Meanwhile, heat 3 tablespoons of the oil in a large skillet over medium-high heat. Add the red, yellow, and green peppers and cook, stirring occasionally, until tender, 6 to 8 minutes. Transfer the peppers to a plate. Set aside.

3. Add the remaining 1 tablespoon oil to the skillet and heat over medium-high heat. Add the sausage and cook until the sausage is cooked through and lightly browned, about 10 minutes. Break up the sausage with the side of a wooden spoon into bite-size pieces as it cooks. Stir in the garlic and red pepper flakes and cook until the garlic is fragrant, about 1 minute. Stir in the peppers and any juices on the plate,

½ cup freshly grated Parmesan cheese, plus more for serving

¼ cup finely chopped fresh basil plus whole leaves for garnish

¼ cup finely chopped fresh flat-leaf parsley

Kosher salt and freshly ground black pepper

scraping up the browned bits in the pan with a wooden spoon. Remove from the heat and cover the skillet with the lid ajar to keep the pepper mixture warm.

4. When the fettuccine is done, scoop out and reserve a half cup of the cooking water. Drain the fettuccine and return to the cooking pot. Add the pepper mixture, Parmesan cheese, basil, and parsley to the pasta and mix well, adding enough of the reserved cooking water to melt the cheese making a creamy sauce. Season with salt and pepper to taste. Spoon into bowls, garnish with the basil leaves, and serve hot, with additional Parmesan passed on the side.

RED-AND-WHITE LASAGNA

MAKES 9 SERVINGS

Many great Italian cooks add besciamella (a creamy white sauce also known in French as béchamel) to their lasagna to give it an extra dose of richness. This is more like a lasagna you would get in Northern Italy, without lots of oregano and garlic in the sauce. Whenever you make lasagna, you might find yourself mumbling "Rome wasn't built in a day." But the results are great and all of the work is done before baking and serving. This is fantastic served as the main course of a buffet with Holiday Chopped Salad (page 58) and Herbed Garlic Bread (page 160).

MEAT SAUCE

2 tablespoons extra-virgin olive oil

¾ pound ground round beef (85% lean)

¾ pound sweet Italian pork sausage, casings removed

1 large yellow onion, chopped

2 garlic cloves, finely chopped

½ teaspoon fennel seeds

1. To make the meat sauce: Heat the oil in a large saucepan over medium-high heat. Add the ground round and sweet Italian sausage and cook until the meat is lightly browned, about 8 minutes. Stir often and break up the meat into small pieces with the side of a wooden spoon. Move the meat to one side of the saucepan. Add the onion, garlic, fennel seeds, and red pepper flakes to the other side of the saucepan and cook until the onion softens, about 2 minutes. Stir the meat and onion mixture together and continue cooking about 3 minutes more.

¼ teaspoon red pepper
flakes

1 cup hearty red wine,
such as a Chianti or
Shiraz

3 cups Rich and Simple
Tomato Sauce (page 131)

Kosher salt and freshly
ground black pepper

BÉCHAMEL
SAUCE

1¾ cups whole milk

¼ cup dry white wine

1 bay leaf

3 tablespoons unsalted
butter

3 tablespoons all-purpose
flour

Pinch of freshly grated
nutmeg

Table salt and freshly
ground black pepper

CHEESE FILLING

4 cups (1 pound)
shredded mozzarella
cheese, preferably fresh
mozzarella (see Note)

One 15-ounce container
ricotta cheese

¼ cup freshly grated
Parmesan cheese

¼ cup finely chopped
fresh flat-leaf parsley

2. Add the wine and bring to a boil, scraping up the browned bits in the saucepan with a wooden spoon. Stir in the tomato sauce. Reduce the heat to medium-low and stir often, until the sauce is slightly reduced, about 45 minutes. Season with salt and pepper to taste. Remove from the heat and let cool slightly.

3. To make the béchamel sauce: Heat the milk, wine, and bay leaf together in a small saucepan over medium heat until bubbles form around the edge of the saucepan. (Or heat the milk mixture in a microwave oven on high for about 2 minutes.) Let stand for 5 minutes. Discard the bay leaf.

4. Melt the butter in a medium heavy-bottom saucepan over medium heat. Whisk in the flour. Reduce the heat to very low and let the mixture bubble without browning for 1 to 2 minutes. Gradually whisk in the milk mixture and bring to a simmer, whisking occasionally, over medium heat. Add the nutmeg and season with salt and pepper to taste. Remove from the heat and cover with the saucepan lid to prevent a skin from forming on the sauce.

5. To make the cheese filling: Mix the mozzarella, ricotta, and Parmesan cheeses with the parsley and eggs.

6. Position a rack in the center of the oven and preheat the oven to 375°F. Spray the inside of a 9 × 13-inch baking dish with the nonstick spray.

2 large eggs, beaten

Nonstick cooking oil spray

8 ounces (12 sheets) oven-ready lasagna sheets

¼ cup freshly grated Parmesan cheese

7. Spread a third of the béchamel sauce in the bottom of the prepared dish. Place 3 lasagna sheets, spaced evenly apart (they should not touch), over the sauce. Spread a third of the meat sauce over the pasta and top with a third of the cheese filling. Repeat twice, finishing with 3 pasta sheets. Cover the top layer, including any exposed filling, with the béchamel sauce and sprinkle with the Parmesan cheese. Spray a sheet of aluminum foil with the nonstick spray and cover the baking dish, oiled side down. Place the baking dish on a large rimmed baking sheet.

8. Bake for 30 minutes. Remove the foil and continue baking until the sauces are bubbling and the béchamel is lightly browned, about 30 minutes more. Let stand for about 15 minutes before cutting and serving.

Note: Fresh mozzarella has a superior flavor to the processed variety, but its soft texture makes it difficult to shred. It helps to freeze the mozzarella for an hour or so until it is very cold but not frozen before shredding. A food processor fitted with the large shredding disk does a good job. Or simply cut the fresh mozzarella into pieces about ½-inch square.

FUSILLI WITH
TOMATO BASIL SAUCE

MAKES 4 TO 6 SERVINGS

Fresh basil, and lots of it, is the key to this incredibly fragrant sauce.

Even though it has a bouillon cube to give it a flavor boost, it is essentially vegetarian, and a nice change from heavy meat sauce, and perfect for a summer dinner. (And you can leave the bouillon cube out.)

Fusilli is a pasta with long, twisty strands that catch the sauce, but any pasta will work with this versatile sauce.

Always add delicate fresh basil to a sauce toward the end of the cooking time so you don't cook away its best features.

4 tablespoons extra-virgin olive oil

8 large button, cremini, or stemmed shiitake mushrooms, thinly sliced

6 large garlic cloves, minced

One 28-ounce can imported Italian tomatoes in juice, preferably San Marzano, puréed in a blender

1 beef or chicken bouillon cube, crushed

1. Heat 2 tablespoons of the olive oil in a large saucepan over medium-high heat. Add the mushrooms and cook, stirring occasionally, until they are lightly browned, about 5 minutes. Reduce the heat to medium-low and stir in the garlic. Cook until the garlic is softened but not browned, about 1 minute. Stir in the tomatoes, beef bouillon cube, and sugar and bring to a boil over high heat. Reduce the heat to medium-low and simmer, stirring occasionally, being sure to dissolve the bouillon cube, until the sauce is slightly reduced, about 30 minutes.

Pinch of sugar

1 pound fusilli, or other long pasta

½ cup finely chopped fresh basil, plus fresh basil leaves for garnish

Kosher salt and freshly ground black pepper

½ cup (4 ounces) freshly grated Parmesan cheese, plus more for serving

2. Meanwhile, bring a large pot of salted water to a boil over high heat. Add the fusilli and cook according to the package directions until al dente. Drain the pasta and return it to the cooking pot.

3. Stir the chopped basil and remaining 2 tablespoons olive oil into the sauce. Season with salt and pepper to taste. Pour the sauce over the pasta, add the Parmesan cheese, and mix well. Transfer to a serving bowl, garnish with the basil leaves, and serve hot, with additional Parmesan cheese served on the side.

PAPPARDELLE WITH
SPRING VEGETABLES

MAKES 4 TO 6 SERVINGS

This recipe uses frozen artichoke hearts, fava beans, and peas for convenience and because they really are excellent. But of course, use fresh if you know how to prep and cook them.

1 pound asparagus, woody stems discarded, stalks cut into 1-inch pieces

2 tablespoons unsalted butter

2 tablespoons extra-virgin olive oil, plus more for serving

1 cup thinly sliced shallots

2 garlic cloves, minced

One 12-ounce bag thawed frozen artichoke hearts

1 cup thawed frozen fava beans (available at Middle Eastern grocers), edamame, or lima beans

1 cup thawed frozen baby green peas

1. Bring a large pot of salted water to a boil over high heat. Add the asparagus and cook just until it is crisp and tender, 3 to 4 minutes. Using a wire sieve, scoop out the asparagus, and rinse the asparagus under cold running water. Drain well. Reduce the heat to medium-low to keep the water simmering.

2. Heat the butter and olive oil together in a large skillet over medium heat. Add the shallots and garlic and cook, stirring often, until they are softened, about 2 minutes. Add the artichoke hearts, fava beans, green peas, and reserved asparagus, and cover. Cook stirring occasionally, until heated through, 3 to 5 minutes. Remove from the heat and season with salt and pepper to taste. Cover the skillet with the lid ajar to keep the vegetables warm.

Kosher salt and freshly
ground black pepper

1 pound pappardelle
or fettuccine

½ cup freshly grated
Parmesan cheese,
plus a chunk of Parmesan
for shaving

3 tablespoons finely
chopped fresh mint

2 tablespoons finely
chopped fresh tarragon

2 tablespoons finely
chopped fresh basil

3. Raise the heat under the water to high. Add the pappardelle and cook according to the package directions until al dente. Reserve 1 cup of the pasta cooking water. Drain the pappardelle well.

4. Return the pappardelle to its cooking pot. Add the vegetable mixture, a half cup shredded Parmesan, mint, tarragon, and basil, and mix, adding enough of the reserved cooking water to make a light and creamy sauce. Season again with salt and pepper. Spoon the pasta into shallow bowls and drizzle with oil. Using a swivel vegetable peeler, shave Parmesan cheese curls on top of each serving. Serve hot.

LISA'S FAMOUS MOSTACCIOLI

MAKES 4 TO 6 SERVINGS

My best friend, Lisa Miles, has been in my life for more than thirty years. And she is one of the most thoughtful, caring, and amazing friends a girl could have. Every single time there has been a milestone in my life, Lisa was there to celebrate. She has baked me this mostaccioli and brought it over to commemorate every special occasion, including the births of each one of my children. Lisa always drops it off when I'm sick or sad, or whenever she knows I'm just too busy to make dinner that night. Her mostaccioli is one of the most delicious meals ever! I'd love to pay this forward, so make some for your family and then you can make it for one of your best friends.

2 pounds ground turkey meat

3 sweet turkey sausages, removed from casing

1 jar Bertolli Olive Oil, Basil, and Garlic Pasta Sauce

One 14.5-ounce can of tomato sauce

One 15-ounce can of chopped tomatoes

One 16-ounce package mostaccioli noodles

1. Preheat the oven to 350°F.

2. Brown the ground turkey meat and sausage in a medium saucepan. Drain the grease and add the Bertolli pasta sauce, tomato sauce, and chopped tomatoes. Let simmer for 15 minutes.

3. While the sauce is simmering, boil the package of mostaccioli noodles and drain.

4. In a large baking dish, combine the noodles and meat sauce.

One 15-ounce container of riccota

One 16-ounce package of mozzarella, thinly sliced

Nonstick cooking oil spray

5. Add in the riccota cheese and mix it all up in the baking dish.

6. Lay the mozzarella slices on top of the pasta and meat sauce mixture.

7. Cover the baking dish with foil (spray the underside of the foil first with cooking oil spray so it doesn't stick to cheese). Bake for 45 minutes. Remove the foil for the last 10 minutes so that the cheese gets a little brown on the top.

PENNE WITH VODKA SAUCE

MAKES 4 TO 6 SERVINGS

The sauce will have the best flavor from the buttery Rich and Simple Tomato Sauce (page 131). If you wish, substitute store-bought marinara sauce, and, if necessary, process it in a blender until smooth.

How does this sauce work? Vodka releases elements in the tomatoes that are only soluble in alcohol. Basically, the advantage to vodka is its lack of flavor, and the tomato taste increases without added flavors of wine, beer, brandy, or other alcoholic beverages.

2 tablespoons unsalted butter

I tablespoon regular olive oil

I teaspoon red pepper flakes

I cup top-quality vodka

3 cups Rich and Simple Tomato Sauce (page 131)

I pound penne or other tubular pasta

¼ cup heavy cream, at room temperature (warmed in a microwave)

1. Heat the butter, olive oil, and red pepper flakes together in a large saucepan over medium heat, just until the pepper flakes release their aroma, about 2 minutes. Add the vodka and bring to a boil over high heat. Boil until the vodka is reduced to a half cup, about 5 minutes.

2. Stir in the tomato sauce and bring to a simmer. Reduce the heat to medium-low and simmer, stirring often, until the sauce is lightly thickened, about 20 minutes.

3. Meanwhile, bring a large pot of salted water to a boil over high heat. Add the penne and cook according to the package

Kosher salt and freshly
ground black pepper

½ cup freshly grated
Parmesan cheese, plus
more for serving

¼ cup finely chopped
fresh flat-leaf parsley

directions until al dente. Drain the pasta well and return it to the cooking pot.

4. Stir the warm cream into the tomato sauce and cook until heated through, about 1 minute. Season with salt and pepper to taste. Pour the sauce over the penne, add the half cup Parmesan cheese, and mix well. Transfer to a serving bowl and sprinkle with the parsley. Serve hot with extra Parmesan served on the side.

RICH AND SIMPLE TOMATO SAUCE

MAKES ABOUT 6 CUPS

There isn't a law that says you must make tomato sauce with olive oil, or that you even have to sauté the onions. In this recipe, butter gives the sauce a creamy richness, and shredded onions melt right into the sauce. Versatile and easy, use it to dress your favorite pasta, or put into action as an ingredient: Red-and-White Lasagna (page 118), Penne with Vodka Sauce (page 129), Spaghetti with Herbed Meatballs (page 137).

This makes about 1½ quarts, enough for 2 pounds of pasta; freeze leftovers for up to 2 months.

Fresh thyme matches well with many foods, but if you want a more Italian flavor, substitute ⅓ cup chopped fresh basil or 3 tablespoons chopped fresh oregano.

Two 28-ounce cans whole peeled Italian plum tomatoes in juice, preferably San Marzano, coarsely chopped, juices reserved

½ cup (1 stick) unsalted butter, cut into tablespoons

1 large yellow onion, shredded on the large holes of a box grater

1. Combine the tomatoes and their juices with the butter, onion, garlic, thyme, bay leaf, and red pepper flakes in a large saucepan. Bring to a boil over medium heat, stirring often. Reduce the heat to low and simmer, stirring often, until the sauce has reduced slightly and the juices have thickened, about 45 minutes. Season with salt and pepper to taste. Let cool slightly.

2. Discard the bay leaf. In batches, process the tomato mixture in a blender with the lid ajar to the desired consistency. Or

3 garlic cloves, finely chopped

1½ teaspoons finely chopped fresh thyme

1 bay leaf

¼ teaspoon red pepper flakes

Kosher salt and freshly ground black pepper

use an immersion blender to process the sauce directly in the saucepan. Use immediately.

Note: The sauce can be cooled, covered, and refrigerated for up to 2 days or frozen for up to 3 months.

WILD MUSHROOM RISOTTO

MAKES 4 SERVINGS

The secret to risotto is stirring. You need to move the rice around in the pot so it releases its starches to give the sauce a naturally creamy consistency. American long-grain rice doesn't have the same starch content as Italian medium grain varieties. Arborio is the most common kind, and most supermarkets carry it now.

1 ounce dried porcini mushrooms

7 cups reduced-sodium chicken broth

3 tablespoons extra-virgin olive oil, plus more for serving

1½ pounds mixed fresh mushrooms, such as white button, cremini, and stemmed shiitake, half thinly sliced, and half chopped

¼ cup finely chopped fresh flat-leaf parsley

2 tablespoons finely chopped fresh tarragon

2 tablespoons finely chopped fresh chives

1. Combine the dried porcini mushrooms and 1 cup of the chicken broth in a small bowl. Let soak until the mushrooms are softened, about 40 minutes. Agitate the mushrooms in the broth to loosen any grit, and lift the mushrooms out of the bowl. Coarsely chop the mushrooms, transfer to another small bowl, and set aside. Strain the mushroom liquid through a wire sieve lined with a moistened paper towel into a third small bowl. Set aside.

2. Heat 1 tablespoon of the oil in a large skillet over medium-high heat. Add the sliced mushrooms and cook, stirring occasionally, until they are lightly browned, 5 to 7 minutes. Stir in the parsley, tarragon, chives, and lemon juice. Season with salt and pepper to taste. Remove the skillet from the heat and cover with its lid to keep the mushrooms warm.

1 tablespoon fresh
lemon juice

Kosher salt and freshly
ground black pepper

1 yellow onion, chopped

1 garlic clove, minced

1 ½ cups Arborio rice

⅔ cup dry white wine

½ cup freshly grated
Parmesan cheese, plus
more for serving

4 tablespoons unsalted
butter, cut into
tablespoons, at room
temperature

3. Bring the remaining 6 cups of broth just to a simmer in a medium saucepan over high heat. Reduce the heat to very low so it is steaming but not simmering.

4. Heat the remaining 2 tablespoons oil in a large heavy-bottomed Dutch oven or saucepan over medium-high heat. Add the chopped mushrooms and cook, stirring occasionally, until their juices have evaporated and they are beginning to brown, 5 to 7 minutes. Stir in the onion and garlic and cook stirring occasionally, until the onions soften, about 3 minutes.

5. Add the rice and reduce the heat to medium. Cook, stirring constantly, until it looks a bit chalky and feels heavier in the spoon, about 2 minutes. (The idea here is to "toast" the rice without browning it.) Stir in the wine and cook, stirring almost constantly, until it has been absorbed by the rice, about 1 minute. Stir in the reserved soaked porcini mushrooms and their soaking liquid and stir until the soaking liquid has been absorbed, about 1 minute more. Stir in a large pinch of salt and a grinding of pepper.

6. Stir in a large ladle (about ¾ cup) of hot broth. Adjust the heat so the risotto is cooking at a steady simmer. Cook, stirring constantly (you can leave the stove for a minute or two, if need be), until just a few tablespoons of broth remain, 2 to 3 minutes. Stir in another ladle of the hot broth, and cook stirring constantly, until it is absorbed, 2 to 3 minutes more. Continue in this manner, adding broth and stirring, until the broth is almost completely absorbed, in 2 to 3 minute

intervals, until the rice is al dente (barely tender with a firm center), for a total of 20 to 25 minutes. If you run out of broth, use hot water. Add the Parmesan and butter and stir until the butter is melted. The risotto should have a loose, spoonable consistency, so stir in more broth (or hot water) as needed. Season with salt and pepper to taste.

7. Spoon the rice into four shallow soup bowls and top with the sliced mushroom mixture. Drizzle each serving with olive oil. Serve hot, with a bowl of Parmesan cheese served on the side.

SPAGHETTI WITH HERBED MEATBALLS

MAKES 4 GENEROUS SERVINGS

This recipe uses Rich and Simple Tomato Sauce. You can also make sliders or hoagies out of the meatballs. Makes 4 generous servings of pasta with 4 meatballs each. Worth making a double batch and freezing half for another meal.

MEATBALLS

1 cup fresh bread crumbs (see Notes)

⅓ cup whole milk

2 large eggs

1 cup (about 4 ounces) very finely chopped (not shredded) Parmesan cheese, prepared in a food processor or blender (see Notes)

¼ cup finely chopped fresh flat-leaf parsley

¼ cup finely chopped fresh chives

1 tablespoon finely chopped fresh thyme

4 garlic cloves, minced

1 teaspoon kosher salt

1. To make the meatballs: In a small bowl, stir the bread crumbs and milk together and let stand for 5 minutes. In a medium bowl, beat the eggs. Drain the bread crumbs in a fine wire sieve and gently press on the bread crumbs to remove the excess milk. Discard the milk. Transfer the softened bread crumbs to the bowl with the eggs. Add the Parmesan cheese, parsley, chives, thyme, garlic, salt, pepper, and red pepper flakes and mix to combine.

2. Crumble the sausage and ground round into the bowl. Using your hands, mix until combined, but do not over mix or the meatballs could be tough. Cover and refrigerate for 30 minutes. Using hands moistened with water, shape the meat mixture into 16 equal balls.

½ teaspoon freshly
ground black pepper

¼ teaspoon red pepper
flakes

I pound sweet
Italian pork sausage,
casings removed
(or a combination of
½ pound each sweet
and hot sausage)

½ pound (85% lean)
ground round

3 tablespoons olive oil,
plus more as needed

SAUCE AND
PASTA

3 cups Rich and Simple
Tomato Sauce (page 131)

I pound spaghetti or
another long pasta

Freshly grated Parmesan
cheese, for serving

3. Heat the olive oil in a large nonstick skillet over medium heat. In batches, adding more oil as needed, cook the meatballs, turning occasionally, until browned on all sides, 6 to 8 minutes. Using a slotted spoon, transfer the meatballs to a plate.

4. Bring the tomato sauce to a simmer in a large saucepan over medium heat. Add the meatballs and return to a simmer. Reduce the heat to low and cover the saucepan. Cook, stirring occasionally and carefully to avoid breaking the meatballs, until the meatballs are cooked through, 15 to 20 minutes.

5. Meanwhile, bring a large pot of salted water to a boil over high heat. Add the spaghetti and cook according to the package directions until al dente. Drain well.

6. Transfer the pasta to a large serving bowl. Add the tomato sauce and meatballs and toss to combine. Serve hot with Parmesan cheese served on the side.

Notes: To make fresh bread crumbs, just process slices of day-old crusty bread in a food processor or blender to make coarse crumbs.

To prepare Parmesan cheese for this recipe, coarsely cut the cheese (without the rind) into 1-inch pieces. Process in a food processor fitted with the metal chopping blade until the cheese is finely chopped to the texture of coarsely ground coffee. Shredded Parmesan is too fine for this recipe, as it melts into the meat mixture during cooking and loses its rough texture.

8. VEGETABLES AND SIDES

SWEET POTATO SOUFFLÉ

MAKES 10 TO 12 SERVINGS

A holiday side dish staple at the Jenner house. For Thanksgiving dinner, here's the only sweet potato dish you'll need!

6 sweet potatoes (not yams)

1 cup (2 sticks) unsalted butter, melted, plus softened butter for ramekins

½ 1 pound box light brown sugar

2 cups white sugar

1 14-ounce can sweetened condensed milk, preferably Eagle brand

1 teaspoon vanilla

1 teaspoon cinnamon

1 teaspoon nutmeg

6 eggs, beaten

1. Preheat oven to 375°F. Lightly butter 2 large ramekins.

2. Quarter the potatoes and boil until soft. Transfer to a large bowl and let cool.

3. When potatoes are cool enough to handle, remove skins and mash with a handheld mixer until smooth.

4. Add melted butter, brown and white sugars, condensed milk, vanilla, cinnamon, and nutmeg to potatoes and blend well.

5. Beat eggs until pale yellow and fold into the potato mixture a third at a time.

6. Pour mixture into the ramekins and bake for about 1 hour. When done, the mixture puffs a little and doesn't wobble when shaken gently.

Serve with fresh whipped cream on the side.

AUNTIE DOROTHY'S ARMENIAN STRING BEANS

Auntie Dorothy would make a double batch for big parties.

These are not supposed to be crisp-tender. The idea is for the beans to soak up flavor from the onion and tomatoes, so they have to cook at least 10 minutes.

¼ cup olive oil

1 medium yellow onion, cut into thin half-moons

1 pound green beans, trimmed, and cut into 1½-inch pieces

One 14-ounce can Italian plum tomatoes in juice, preferably San Marzano, coarsely chopped and juices reserved

Kosher salt and freshly ground black pepper

1. Heat the olive oil in a large saucepan over medium heat. Add the onion and cook, stirring often, until the onion is softened, about 3 minutes.

2. Stir in the green beans, the tomatoes, and their juices and bring to a boil over medium heat. Reduce the heat to medium-low and cover. Cook at a brisk simmer, stirring often, until the beans are tender and the tomato juices have thickened, 10 to 15 minutes. Season with salt and pepper to taste.

LARGE-BATCH ARMENIAN GREEN BEANS

Use ½ cup olive oil, 1 large yellow onion, 2 pounds green beans, and one 28-ounce can plum tomatoes in juice.

ROASTED BRUSSELS SPROUTS

MAKES 6 SERVINGS

Roasting brings out the flavor of the Brussels sprouts. This version has a very simple glaze that takes a good thing and makes it better. Terrific for a holiday meal and easy enough for a weeknight.

Three 10-ounce containers Brussels sprouts, bottoms trimmed

6 tablespoons (¾ stick) unsalted butter, melted

⅓ cup plus 1 tablespoon dry white wine

1½ tablespoons Worcestershire sauce

1½ tablespoons sugar

1 tablespoon finely chopped fresh thyme

Kosher salt and freshly ground black pepper

1. Bring a large pot of salted water to a boil over high heat. Add the Brussels sprouts and cook until they have softened slightly and are a brighter shade of green, about 5 minutes. Drain and rinse well under cold water. Cut the sprouts in half lengthwise and pat dry with paper towels. The sprouts can be refrigerated in plastic storage bags for 1 day.

2. Preheat the oven to 450°F.

3. Toss the sprouts, melted butter, wine, Worcestershire sauce, sugar, and thyme in a 10 × 15-inch glass or ceramic baking dish and spread the sprouts in a single layer. Bake, stirring occasionally, until the mixture is almost completely evaporated and the sprouts are tender and golden brown, 20 to 25 minutes. Season with salt and pepper to taste. Transfer to a serving dish and serve immediately.

TRUFFLED CAULIFLOWER MASH

MAKES 8 TO 10 SERVINGS

This is the Neiman Marcus version of mashed potatoes. It's very special and expensive but worth every penny. You won't be putting gravy on these. If you wish, substitute a 3-ounce container of white truffle butter for the unsalted butter and omit the truffle oil. Do not use an immersion "stick" blender to purée the cauliflower—there's too much volume for this kind of blender. If you don't have a processor, purée the leek mixture with most of the cream in a stand blender. Mash the cauliflower, leek mixture, and truffle oil with a handheld electric mixer (it will be a little chunky, but that's okay). Add more cream as needed.

3 heads cauliflower, broken into large florets

6 tablespoons unsalted butter

4 leeks (2 cups), white and pale green parts only, chopped and well rinsed

6 garlic cloves, minced

1 tablespoon finely chopped fresh thyme

Kosher salt and freshly ground black pepper

1. Bring a large pot of salted water to a boil over high heat. Add the cauliflower and reduce the heat to medium. Cook until the cauliflower is very tender, about 15 minutes. Drain well. Return the cauliflower to the pot and cook over low heat, stirring almost constantly, to evaporate some of the excess moisture from the cauliflower, about 2 minutes.

2. Meanwhile, melt the butter in a large skillet over medium heat. Add the leeks and garlic and cook, stirring often, until the leeks are tender, about 5 minutes. Stir in the thyme and

2 tablespoons white truffle oil

½ cup heavy cream, heated to steaming, as needed

season with salt and pepper to taste. Remove from the heat and cover with the lid to keep warm.

3. Transfer the cauliflower, the leek mixture, and the truffle oil to a food processor. Process the mixture until smooth, adding enough of the heavy cream through the feed tube to give the mash the consistency of soft mashed potatoes. Season with salt and pepper to taste. Transfer to a serving bowl and serve hot. The purée can be made up to 2 hours ahead and reheated in a large skillet over medium-low heat.

NANA'S "WEDDING" RICE PILAF

MAKES 8 TO 10 SERVINGS

We've all heard of family heirloom jewelry—the kind that is passed down from one generation to the next. Nana's rice pilaf is a family heirloom recipe. I got it from Robert's mother, Helen Kardashian, and it's truly special.

When I make this dish, I cannot describe how I feel just thinking of Nana. Just shopping for the ingredients gives me joy because it reminds me of the power of family love—and family legend (more on this later).

In Nana's world there was no such thing as too much food. She would often host the family dinners. There would be so many dishes piled on the table it would be, literally, overflowing. One day, I suggested she might want to think about scaling back on the food. Why did I do that? Nana looked at me as if I'd said Robert and I were going to put her grandchildren up for adoption.

Not long after that brunch I found out why. In Armenian culture, Nana later explained to me, food equals love. The more food an Armenian hostess serves, the more she is said to love her guests. And Nana *adored* hers; she didn't just cover her table with food, she piled dishes on top of one another when she ran out of room!

Although I learned to cook this particular dish from Nana, the place where we grew to love it was at big Armenian weddings. Kardashian family tradition holds that a bride who serves Armenian rice pilaf at her wedding will know great love and wealth. Can I swear the legend is true? No, I can't. But I *can* swear to this: The recipe is delicious— over-the-moon good.

It's one of those dishes that blends families (Robert's and mine) and cultures

(Armenian and American) and generations (Kourtney, Kim, and Khloé make it just like their grandmother—with clarified butter—and Rob loves it!).

The "wedding" version is what I serve at big family gatherings, just like Nana did. The "everyday" version (sans raisins, almonds, and dates), I cook on any given weeknight. For an authentic Kardashian culinary experience, serve it with Armenian Lamb Shish Kebabs (page 87).

And, if there's a family wedding in your future, give Nana's recipe to the caterer and insist it be followed *to the letter*!

You can easily halve the recipe, cooking in a smaller saucepan, for 4 to 5 servings.

This is a typical Armenian recipe. The raisins and almonds are usually only added to the plain pilaf for special occasions (when it is called "Wedding Pilaf"), but it doesn't take much effort, even for weeknight cooking.

½ cup blanched slivered almonds

3 tablespoons clarified butter (page 15)
or unsalted butter

1½ cups vermicelli, broken into 1½- to 2-inch pieces

2 cups long-grain rice

3½ cups reduced-sodium chicken broth, heated to steaming

1½ teaspoons kosher salt

¼ teaspoon freshly ground black pepper

½ cup seedless raisins

1. Heat a medium skillet over medium heat. Add the almonds and cook, stirring occasionally, until toasted, about 3 minutes. Transfer the almonds to a plate. Set aside.

2. Heat the clarified butter in a medium saucepan over medium heat. Add the vermicelli and stir constantly until it is lightly toasted, about 1 minute. Add the rice and stir constantly until most of the rice turns chalky white, about 1 minute more. Add the chicken broth, salt, and pepper and bring to a boil over high heat. Reduce the heat to medium-low and cover the saucepan tightly. Simmer until the rice is tender and has absorbed the liquid, about 18 minutes.

3. Remove from the heat. Add the toasted almonds and raisins (do not stir them in) and cover the saucepan again. Let stand for 5 minutes. Fluff the pilaf with a fork and transfer to a serving bowl. Serve hot.

GRILLED EGGPLANT WITH SCALLIONS AND GARLIC

MAKES 8 SERVINGS

An easy grilled dish that does well with lots of main courses such as Armenian Shish Kebabs (page 87), simple steaks, and chops. This is all about the eggplant, so pick them carefully. Get firm and unblemished eggplants with tight, shiny skin. Leftovers? Dress with vinaigrette and serve as a salad.

2 globe eggplants, trimmed, cut into ½-inch-thick rounds

½ cup extra-virgin olive oil

1 tablespoon kosher salt

¾ teaspoon freshly ground black pepper

4 scallions, white and green parts

2 garlic cloves, peeled

1. Brush the eggplant rounds on both sides with the olive oil. Mix the salt and pepper together, and use the mixture to season the eggplant on both sides. Place the eggplant, overlapping as needed, in a very large glass or ceramic baking dish. Finely chop the scallions and garlic together on a chopping board. Transfer half of the scallion mixture to a bowl, cover tightly with plastic wrap, and refrigerate. Rub the remaining scallion mixture all over the eggplants. Cover and let stand at room temperature for at least 2 hours and up to 4.

2. Prepare an outdoor grill for direct cooking over medium heat. Brush the grill grate clean. For a charcoal grill, let the coals burn until covered with white ash and you can hold your hand just above the grill grates for 3 to 4 seconds. For

a gas grill, preheat the grill on High, then adjust the heat to 400°F.

3. Place the eggplant on the grill. Keeping the grill lid closed as much as possible, cook until the undersides are golden brown, about 5 minutes. Turn the eggplant over and continue cooking, with the grill closed, until tender, 4 to 5 minutes more. Transfer the eggplant to a serving dish. Sprinkle with the reserved scallion mixture and serve hot.

WILD MUSHROOM STUFFING

MAKES 12 TO 16 SERVINGS

This is *not* Grandma's stuffing. Rich, satisfying, full of flavor, but not so "chef-y" that it will raise eyebrows. You will need to cook the mushroom mixture in two batches, as even the largest sauté pan cannot hold all of the ingredients in a single go. You can do this the night before to get it out of the way. Don't make the entire stuffing the night before, because refrigerator-cold stuffing takes forever to heat up inside of the bird. Also, remember that you can only stuff so much dressing into a turkey, and that you will always have extra to bake on the side. Never cram stuffing inside of the bird, as it expands during baking when it soaks up the turkey juices. If you wish, add 1 pound sliced bacon, cooked until crisp and coarsely chopped, to the stuffing when mixing. It's totally extra, but a nice addition if you want to go over the top.

2 ounces dried porcini mushrooms, quickly rinsed under cold water

1 cup dry white wine

12 tablespoons (1½ sticks) unsalted butter, divided, plus softened butter for the baking dish

1. The night before serving the stuffing, combine the dried mushrooms and wine in a small bowl. Let soak until the mushrooms are softened, about 40 minutes. Agitate the mushrooms in the wine to loosen any grit, and lift the mushrooms out of the bowl. Coarsely chop the mushrooms and transfer to another small bowl. Set aside. Strain the soaking liquid through a wire sieve lined with a moistened paper towel into another small bowl. Set aside.

1½ pounds mixed fresh mushrooms, such as white button, cremini, and stemmed shiitake, coarsely chopped

1 cup chopped shallots

2 medium leeks, white and pale green parts only, thinly sliced and well rinsed

4 celery ribs, cut into ½-inch dice

4 garlic cloves, minced

3–4 cups reduced-sodium chicken broth, as needed

Kosher salt and freshly ground black pepper

One loaf rustic bread, about 1⅓ pounds, bought the day before making the stuffing, and cut into 1-inch cubes

1 cup heavy cream

¾ cup finely chopped fresh flat-leaf parsley

2 tablespoons finely chopped fresh thyme

2 tablespoons finely chopped fresh sage

2 tablespoons white truffle oil

3 large eggs, beaten

2. Melt 6 tablespoons of the butter in a very large skillet over medium-high heat. Add half of the fresh mushrooms and cook 3 to 4 minutes, stirring occasionally, until their liquid has evaporated and they are beginning to brown. Push the mushrooms to one side of the skillet, and add half of the shallots, leeks, celery, garlic, and soaked mushrooms to the empty side. Let cook until the shallots soften, about 1 minute. Mix the shallot mixture with the mushrooms and continue to cook until the celery softens, about 3 minutes more. Add 1 cup of the broth and half of the reserved soaking liquid and bring to a simmer. Cook, stirring occasionally, until the liquid has reduced by about half, 8 to 10 minutes. Transfer the mushroom mixture to a large bowl. Repeat with the remaining butter, fresh mushrooms, shallots, leeks, celery, garlic, soaked mushrooms, remaining soaking liquid, and 1 cup of broth. Transfer to the bowl. Season with salt and pepper to taste. The mushroom mixture can be cooled, transferred to 1-gallon plastic storage bags, and refrigerated overnight. Reheat the mushroom mixture in a large nonstick skillet over medium heat before using.

3. Add the bread cubes, cream, parsley, thyme, sage, and truffle oil to the mushroom mixture and mix well. Season with salt and pepper to taste. Mix in the beaten eggs and enough of the remaining broth (about a half cup, or more if the mushroom mixture was refrigerated) to give the stuffing a moist, but not wet, consistency.

4. Use immediately as a turkey stuffing. Spread any remaining stuffing in a buttered shallow baking dish, cover with

aluminum foil, and refrigerate until ready to bake and serve. Before serving, drizzle the stuffing with about a half cup of the remaining broth and bake covered with foil in a pre-heated 350°F oven until warm, 20 to 30 minutes depending on the size of the baking dish. Remove the foil and continue baking until the top is crisp and the stuffing is hot, about 15 minutes. Let stand for 5 minutes before serving.

SPICY SWEET POTATO STEAK FRIES

MAKES 4 SERVINGS

When the need to indulge hits, some people go for comfort food (chicken and waffle sliders!), others go for something fancier (Champagne and caviar). I love both. But I'm always on the lookout for figure-friendly options. My current obsession: these no-fry fries. They're divine. The outside is crunchy, the inside is creamy. And, unless you eat the whole pan, they're as close to guilt-free as you can get!

This is an easy side dish for a busy weeknight. Thick, not skinny, fries. Do not crowd the sweet potato wedges or their steam will keep them from browning properly.

1½ pounds orange-fleshed sweet potatoes, peeled and cut lengthwise into eighths

2 tablespoons olive oil

½ teaspoon kosher salt

½ teaspoon ground cumin

½ teaspoon chili powder

¼ teaspoon garlic powder

⅛ teaspoon cayenne pepper

1. Position a rack in the top third of the oven and preheat the oven to 450°F.

2. Toss the sweet potato wedges with the olive oil on a large rimmed baking sheet, coating them evenly. Spread the wedges out in a single layer on the baking sheet, making sure that they don't touch one another. Roast, flipping the fries after 10 minutes, until browned and tender, about 25 minutes. Remove from the oven.

3. Mix the salt, cumin, chili powder, garlic powder, and cayenne together. Sprinkle the spice mixture evenly over the wedges on the baking sheet, turning them a few times to coat evenly. Serve hot.

CRÈME SPINACH PIE

MAKES 6 SERVINGS

Sheila and Samantha Kolker are lifelong family friends. I get a lot of my recipes from my friends. It's like one huge Valentine to share recipes. And it's the biggest compliment when someone eats your food and they love it so much that they want to re-create it.

I have no shame in asking someone for their recipe when they have made something that is truly delicious. Well, this is one of those dishes. And Sheila and Samantha were gracious enough to share it!

Note: The key to this dish is you want the filling to be thick and not too wet. Make sure to remove water from your thawed frozen spinach before cooking it.

1 round premade refrigerated pie dough

3 tablespoons unsalted butter

1 medium yellow onion, finely chopped

2 garlic cloves, minced

¼ cup all-purpose flour

2¼ cups whole milk

1. Preheat the oven to 400°F.

2. Line a 9-inch pie pan with the pie dough. Prick the dough with a fork. Line the dough with a sheet of aluminum foil and fill with pie weights or a handful of dried beans. Bake until the dough under the foil looks set, 12 to 15 minutes. Lift up and remove the foil with the weights. Continue baking until the piecrust is lightly browned, 10 to 15 minutes more. Remove from the oven. Keep the oven on.

1½ pounds thawed frozen chopped spinach (from 1½ one-pound bags)

1 tablespoon olive oil

Kosher salt and freshly ground black pepper

½ cup shredded Gruyère or Swiss cheese (2 ounces)

One 2.8-ounce can french-fried onions

3. Meanwhile, melt the butter in a medium saucepan over medium heat. Add the onion and garlic and cook, stirring occasionally, until tender but not browned, about 4 minutes. Sprinkle with the flour and stir well. Gradually stir in the milk and bring to a simmer. Reduce the heat to low and simmer, stirring occasionally, until the sauce is thick, about 5 minutes. Remove the sauce from the heat.

4. Drain the thawed spinach in a colander. A handful at a time, squeeze the spinach well to remove the excess water and transfer the spinach to a large bowl. You should have 1½ packed cups. Heat the oil in a large nonstick skillet over medium-high heat. Add the spinach and cook, stirring often, to evaporate any remaining water, about 2 minutes. Stir into the sauce. Season to taste with salt and pepper. Pour into the pie shell. Sprinkle the Gruyère on top.

5. Bake until the Gruyère is lightly browned, about 20 minutes. Remove from the oven. Immediately sprinkle the fried onions on top so they adhere to the melted cheese. Let the pie cool about 10 minutes. Slice the pie and serve it warm.

CRANBERRY ORANGE RELISH WITH MAPLE SYRUP AND GRAND MARNIER

You can add ¼ cup finely chopped crystallized ginger to this. Use fresh cranberries in season, but this works perfectly with frozen; do not thaw the frozen cranberries. Grade B syrup is not inferior to Grade A—it is just thicker and has more maple flavor, so it is good for cooking. If you only have Grade A, and want a strong maple flavor, add ¼ teaspoon maple extract (or more to taste) to the sauce near the end of cooking. I always make cranberry sauce from scratch—it is easy and much better than the canned stuff.

1 large navel orange

One 12-ounce bag fresh or frozen cranberries

½ cup sugar

½ cup maple syrup, preferably Grade B

¼ cup orange-flavored liqueur, preferably Grand Marnier

1. Finely grate the zest from the orange and reserve the zest. Cut the rind from the orange where it meets the flesh. Working over a bowl, cut between the orange membranes to release the orange sections into a bowl. Discard the orange membranes.

2. Combine the cranberries, sugar, maple syrup, and liqueur with the orange zest and sections in a medium heavy-bottom saucepan. Bring to a boil over medium-high heat, stirring often. Reduce the heat to medium and cook at a strong simmer, stirring often, until the cranberries have all popped and the liquid is reduced by about a third, about 10 minutes.

3. This makes a fairly loose sauce. If you want a firmer sauce, cook 12 to 15 minutes or until the liquid is reduced by about half and has a syrupy consistency. Transfer to a bowl and let cool. Cover and refrigerate for at least 2 hours, until chilled.

Note: The sauce can be refrigerated for up to 1 week.

HERBED GARLIC BREAD

MAKES 8 TO 12 SERVINGS

Everyone has a garlic bread recipe. It's the perfect complement to any pasta dish. I upgrade mine with lots of herbs from the garden and fresh garlic.

6 garlic cloves, minced

2 teaspoons olive oil

4 tablespoons (½ stick) unsalted butter, at room temperature

¼ cup freshly grated Parmesan cheese

¼ cup finely chopped fresh flat-leaf parsley

2 tablespoons finely chopped fresh oregano

2 teaspoons finely chopped fresh thyme

Kosher salt and freshly ground black pepper

1 large, elongated crusty bread, such as ciabatta, cut in half horizontally

1. Preheat oven to 350°F.

2. Heat the garlic and olive oil together in a small skillet over medium-low heat, stirring occasionally, until the garlic is tender but not browned, about 2 minutes. Scrape the mixture into a medium bowl and let cool completely.

3. In a medium bowl, combine the butter, Parmesan, parsley, oregano, and thyme. Using a rubber spatula, mash the mixture together until combined. Season with salt and pepper to taste. Divide and spread the herb mixture on the cut sides of the bread. Wrap the loaf in a double thickness of aluminum foil.

4. Bake for 20 minutes. Open up the foil and continue baking until the loaf is crisp, about 5 minutes. Cut into 1-inch-wide slices and serve warm.

QUICK CHEESE ROLLS

MAKES 8 SERVINGS

This is a fast side dish. Broiled, not baked. Use your favorite cheese (Cheddar or Swiss) instead of mozzarella. You can even put sliced tomatoes on the rolls (before adding the cheese mixture) to make quick pizzas.

½ cup (1 stick) unsalted butter, at room temperature

3 garlic cloves, minced

4 large, crusty rolls, preferably sourdough, cut in half crosswise

1 cup shredded or finely chopped fresh mozzarella cheese

½ cup freshly grated Parmesan cheese

1. Position a broiler rack about 6 inches from the source of heat and preheat the broiler on high.

2. In a small bowl, mash the butter and garlic together. Spread the cut surfaces of the rolls with the garlic butter. Mix the mozzarella and Parmesan cheeses together and sprinkle over the rolls.

3. Broil the rolls until the cheese is melted and the bread is toasted around the edges, 1 to 2 minutes. Serve immediately.

HERBED SOURDOUGH BREAD

MAKES 8 TO 12 SERVINGS

Some of my fondest memories involve hanging out with one of my best friends, Shelli Azoff, and raising our kids together. I am so excited to share this French bread recipe with you because we just couldn't keep our hands off it!

1 cup (2 sticks) unsalted butter, at room temperature

½ cup freshly grated Parmesan cheese

⅓ cup finely chopped fresh chives

⅓ cup finely chopped fresh flat-leaf parsley

½ teaspoon dried thyme

½ teaspoon garlic salt

¼ teaspoon freshly ground black pepper

1 long loaf sourdough bread (about 15 ounces)

1. Preheat the oven to 400°F.

2. Mash the butter, Parmesan, chives, parsley, thyme, garlic salt, and pepper together in a small bowl.

3. Using a serrated knife, cut the bread in half lengthwise. Spread the butter mixture on cut surfaces of the bread. Sandwich the halves together. Turn the bread on its side and cut it crosswise into 1-inch slices, being sure not to cut all the way through the bread. Wrap the loaf in aluminum foil.

4. Bake until the bread is heated through and the butter has melted, about 25 minutes. Serve warm.

9. DESSERTS AND BAKED GOODS

LEMON CHIFFON PIE

MAKES 8 SERVINGS

This is the first complicated dessert I ever learned to make. After I mastered brownies, I was so proud to even attempt this one. I followed the recipe to a T and it turned out perfect—creamy, tart, sweet, and delicious. There is nothing better than a homemade graham cracker crust and mixed with the tartness of the lemon, there simply isn't anything like it.

Robert Kardashian loved anything lemon, so I couldn't wait to try this recipe. And after the first time I made it, he couldn't wait to come home from a busy day at work and see this waiting for him for dessert. He would be so excited. And I was so happy. I was very young when we got married, but making this dessert for him made me feel very grown-up.

Every time I make this pie, it reminds me of having all of my babies running around as I was trying to assemble everything and keep up with them. It was hectic, but so worth it.

Note: You can substitute limes for a lime chiffon pie. This is a good pie to make in the winter when berries aren't around but there is plenty of citrus at the market.

GRAHAM CRACKER CRUST

3 tablespoons unsalted butter, melted, plus more, softened for pie pan

1 ¼ cups (9 whole crackers) graham cracker crumbs

2 tablespoons granulated sugar

FILLING

1 ½ teaspoons plain powdered gelatin

¼ cup cold water

4 large eggs, separated, at room temperature

1 cup sugar, divided

Finely grated zest of 2 lemons

½ cup fresh lemon juice

Pinch of salt

WHIPPED CREAM

1 cup heavy cream

4 teaspoons confectioners' sugar

1. Preheat the oven to 350°F. Lightly butter a 9-inch pie pan.

2. To make the crust: In a medium bowl, mix together the graham cracker crumbs, melted butter, and granulated sugar until the crumbs are evenly moistened. Press the crumbs firmly and evenly onto the bottom and up the sides of the prepared pie pan. Bake until the crust looks lightly toasted, about 15 minutes. Cool completely.

3. To make the filling: Sprinkle the gelatin over the water in a small bowl. Set aside.

4. In a heatproof medium bowl, whisk together the egg yolks and a half cup of the sugar until thick and lemon colored. Whisk in the lemon zest, lemon juice, and the salt.

5. Place the bowl over a saucepan of briskly simmering water (the bottom of the bowl should not touch the water). Whisk constantly until the sugar is dissolved. With a rubber spatula, stir the lemon mixture, scraping down the sides of the bowl, until it thickens and reads 185°F on an instant-read thermometer, 5 to 7 minutes. It should be thick enough that your finger will cut a swath when you run it over the mixture on the spatula. Remove from the heat, add the gelatin mixture, and stir well to completely dissolve the gelatin.

6. Strain the lemon mixture through a wire sieve into another medium bowl set in a larger bowl of iced water. Let stand, stirring often, until the mixture is chilled and beginning to set, about 10 minutes.

7. Using an electric mixer set on high speed, whip the egg whites until foamy. Gradually beat in the remaining half cup sugar and continue whipping the whites until they form stiff, shiny peaks. Fold about a third of the whites into the lemon mixture to lighten it, then fold in the remaining whites. Pour the filling into the graham cracker shell. Refrigerate until the filling is completely chilled and set, at least 2 hours.

8. To make the whipped cream: Using an electric mixer set on high speed, beat the heavy cream and confectioners' sugar until stiff.

9. Cut the pie into wedges and serve chilled, with dollops of the whipped cream.

BERRY CRUMBLE

MAKES 4 INDIVIDUAL SERVINGS

You can use any berries that you like but this is a good combination. Strawberries lose some of their color and flavor when cooked, so they aren't good unless mixed with darker berries that give off colored juices.

I bake this in individual servings, which is nice for parties. But for a family dessert, it can also be baked in an 8 × 11.5-inch baking dish for about 30 minutes.

Try to serve warm, but these are great at room temperature, too. Just don't reheat them in the microwave, or the crumble topping will get soggy.

Fruit crumbles are popular because they are so delicious . . . and easy. Apples, pears, plums, peaches, nectarines, cherries . . . they all make great crisps. Just use 5 to 6 cups of prepared (pitted, cored, peeled, sliced, what-have-you) fruit.

TOPPING

½ cup all-purpose flour

¼ cup packed light brown sugar

½ cup granola (any flavor)

½ teaspoon ground cinnamon

1. Position a rack in the center of the oven and preheat the oven to 350°F. Lightly butter four 1¼-cup (10 ounce) custard cups or ramekins.

2. To make the topping: In a medium bowl, mix together the flour, brown sugar, granola, and cinnamon. Add the butter and use your fingertips to rub it into the flour mixture until the topping is combined and crumbly. Set aside.

5 tablespoons (½ stick plus 1 tablespoon) cold unsalted butter, cut into ½-inch cubes

FILLING

½ cup granulated sugar

2 tablespoons cornstarch

1 pint fresh blueberries

½ pint fresh raspberries

½ pint fresh blackberries

Grated zest of 1 lemon

1 tablespoon fresh lemon juice

Softened butter, for the baking dishes

Vanilla ice cream or whipped cream (page 167), for serving

3. To make the filling: In a large bowl, whisk together the granulated sugar and cornstarch. Add the blueberries, raspberries, blackberries, lemon zest and juice, and toss gently to coat the berries. Divide the berry mixture evenly among the prepared custard cups. Crumble the topping over the berry mixture.

4. Place the custard cups on a large rimmed baking sheet and bake until the topping is lightly browned and the berry juices are bubbling, about 35 minutes. Let cool for at least 15 minutes.

5. Serve warm, adding a scoop of ice cream to each crumble.

MAGIC COOKIE BARS

MAKES 24 BARS

This recipe has been around forever. It's an oldie, but it's a goodie. I love it the way I loved Vienna Finger cookies when I was pregnant with Kourtney: way too much. In my second trimester, I ate them by the boxful. By the end of my seventh month, I'd put on so much weight, Robert sat me down and gently suggested I limit myself to a few boxes a week. Of course, I didn't listen. And I gained fifty pounds.

And not just with Kourtney. With Kim and Khloé, too, although my cravings were totally different. With Kim, I was obsessed with oranges. With Khloé, it was all about the Cheesecake Factory's blue cheese dressing. (With Rob, I didn't have any cravings and kept my weight gain to 30 pounds. Go figure; must have been a pregnant-with-a-girl-baby thing.) But when I was pregnant with Kourtney, I couldn't get enough of Vienna Fingers. Unfortunately, in my seventh month, my cravings turned into a full-on addiction, an addiction that I went to great lengths to hide. At night, as soon as Robert fell asleep, I'd lock myself in the pantry and eat myself into Vienna Finger bliss. He only caught me once, which is pretty remarkable when you consider how much I indulged.

Recently, I developed an equally strong craving for these Magic Cookie Bars. Hmm.

This recipe is also sometimes called Hello Dolly Bars or Seven-Layer Cookies. You may have a similar recipe, but this one is so good and easy to make.

Nonstick cooking oil spray, for the baking pan

1 ½ cups graham cracker crumbs

½ cup (1 stick) unsalted butter, melted

1 cup (6 ounces) semisweet chocolate chips

One 3-ounce bittersweet chocolate bar, cut into ½-inch chunks

1 cup (6 ounces) butterscotch or peanut butter chips

1 ⅓ cups sweetened coconut flakes

1 cup (4 ounces) chopped pecans

One 14-ounce can sweetened condensed milk

1. Position a rack in the center of the oven and preheat the oven to 350°F. Spray a 9 × 13-inch baking dish with the cooking spray.

2. In a medium bowl, mix together the graham cracker crumbs and butter to thoroughly moisten the crumbs. Press the mixture firmly and evenly into the prepared baking pan.

3. Sprinkle the semisweet chocolate chips, bittersweet chocolate, butterscotch chips, coconut flakes, and pecans over the graham cracker crust, then drizzle evenly with the condensed milk.

4. Bake until the coconut flakes are lightly browned, 20 to 25 minutes. Transfer to a wire cooling rack and let cool completely in the pan. Run a knife around the edges of the pan, and cut into 24 bars. Remove from the pan.

Note: The bars can be stored in an airtight container at room temperature for up to five days.

BROWNIES

MAKES 20 BROWNIES

I don't just like these brownies, I love them. They're a sentimental favorite for a couple of reasons. This is the first recipe I learned at the culinary school. And they're Rob's favorite.

I probably shouldn't have, but when Rob graduated from USC I baked him two pans. I'd already thrown him a fabulous celebration at the Polo Lounge, but nothing says "I love you" to my only son quite like these brownies.

When they're fresh out of the oven, they're divine. Add homemade whipped cream for a truly heavenly experience.

These are one-pot brownies—choose a saucepan that is big enough for mixing the batter. But I also like making them in a food processor. These are delicious and chewy. I usually bake more than I need and freeze them. Serve with vanilla ice cream and enjoy!!!

Crisco white shortening, for pans

1 cup (2 sticks) unsalted butter, cubed

4 ounces unsweetened chocolate, coarsely chopped, preferably Baker's brand

1 cup all-purpose flour

1. Position a rack in the center of the oven and preheat the oven to 325°F. Grease a 9 × 13-inch baking pan with Crisco.

2. Melt the butter in a large saucepan over medium heat. Remove from the heat. Add the unsweetened chocolate and let stand until the chocolate looks softened, about 3 minutes. Stir well until the chocolate is completely melted. Let cool slightly for 5 minutes.

½ teaspoon baking powder

½ teaspoon salt

2 cups sugar

4 large eggs, at room temperature

2 teaspoons vanilla extract

2 cups (12 ounces) mini semisweet chocolate chips

1 cup coarsely chopped walnuts, optional

3. In a large bowl, mix together the flour, baking powder, and salt. Set aside.

4. In a large bowl, whisk the sugar into the chocolate mixture. Whisk in the eggs, 1 at a time. Whisk in the vanilla. Fold in the flour mixture and stir (do not whisk) until combined. Stir in the semisweet chocolate chips and walnuts. Pour the batter into the prepared baking pan and smooth the top with an offset spatula.

5. Bake until a wooden toothpick inserted in the center of the brownie comes out clean, about 23 minutes. Transfer to a wire cooling rack and let cool for 10 minutes. Run a knife around the edges of the pan to release the brownie from the sides, then let cool completely in the pan.

6. Cut into 20 squares. Remove the brownies from the pan. Separate the brownies and serve.

Note: The brownies can be stored in an airtight container at room temperature for up to 5 days.

FOOD PROCESSOR BROWNIES

1. Combine butter and the unsweetened chocolate, broken into pieces, in a Pyrex measuring cup and melt for 2½ minutes in the microwave. Stir and set aside.

2. Blend the eggs and vanilla in a food processor.

3. Add through the tube the sugar, salt, baking powder, and flour.

4. Slowly add the chocolate and butter mixture through the tube.

5. Mix in processor for 2 minutes.

6. Pour into processor one 12-ounce bag of mini semisweet chocolate chips and pulse until blended.

7. Pour into greased pan and bake for 23 minutes.

BERRY COBBLER

MAKES 6 SERVINGS

I have been making this dessert since the dawn of time. And I find myself making it more frequently in the summer months when the berries are so fresh and sweet and delicious. This is great for big groups or if you look up and there are twenty people hanging out at your house because it's so quick to make. As long as I have a basket of berries in the fridge, I can throw this together in 10 minutes. And it holds well. You can keep it in the fridge and pop it in the oven and it tastes as if you have been cooking it all day.

This cobbler topping is cakelike, thanks to the egg. And there's just enough cornstarch in the filling to help thicken the juices.

FILLING

Three 6-ounce containers fresh blackberries

Three 6-ounce containers fresh blueberries

Three 6-ounce containers fresh raspberries

½ cup granulated sugar

½ cup packed light brown sugar

2 tablespoons cornstarch

1. To make the filling: In a large bowl, mix together the blackberries, blueberries, raspberries, granulated sugar, brown sugar, cornstarch, and cinnamon. Making sure not to bruise the berries. Let stand for about 30 minutes.

2. Preheat the oven to 350°F. Butter a 9 × 13-inch baking dish.

3. To make the topping: In a medium bowl, whisk together the flour, granulated sugar, baking powder, and salt. Add the butter and toss to coat with the flour mixture. Using a pastry blender or two knives, cut in the butter until the mixture

1 teaspoon ground
cinnamon

Softened butter, for
the baking dish

TOPPING

2 cups unbleached
all-purpose flour

⅓ cup plus 1 tablespoon
granulated sugar

1 tablespoon baking
powder

½ teaspoon salt

½ cup (1 stick) cold
unsalted butter, cut
into small cubes

1 cup heavy cream

1 large egg, beaten

2 tablespoons coarse
sugar, such as raw
or Demerara

resembles coarse crumbs with some pea-size pieces of butter. Mix the cream and egg together in a measuring cup. Stir into the flour mixture, just until combined.

4. Pour the filling into the baking dish. Spoon six large dollops of the topping, evenly spaced, over the filling. Sprinkle with the coarse sugar.

5. Place the dish on a baking sheet and bake until the topping is golden brown and the filling is bubbling, about 40 minutes. Loosely cover the topping with aluminum foil if it browns too quickly. Serve warm or at room temperature.

KIM'S PUMPKIN BREAD

MAKES 8 SERVINGS

Kim doesn't make this recipe, but she's the reason I do. Her birthday is around Halloween so there is always a pumpkin theme happening during that time of year. When she was in middle school, she brought this bread home from an eighth-grade holiday recipe swap. It was fabulous. So fabulous that at Christmas, I make it for my closest girlfriends.

This bread keeps very well, wrapped in plastic wrap, at room temperature. Be sure to use plain pumpkin purée, and not pumpkin pie filling (which has already been seasoned).

Large quick breads like this one are too big to test with a toothpick, so use a long bamboo skewer (the kind some people use for grilling) instead.

Softened butter for the pan

3½ cups all-purpose flour, plus more for dusting the pan

3 cups sugar

2 teaspoons salt

2 teaspoons baking soda

1 teaspoon ground allspice

1. Position a rack in the center of the oven and preheat the oven to 350°F. Lightly butter and flour a 9 × 5 × 3-inch loaf pan, tapping out the excess flour.

2. In a medium bowl, sift together the flour, sugar, salt, baking soda, allspice, cinnamon, cloves, and baking powder.

3. In a large bowl, whisk together the pumpkin, vegetable oil, eggs, and water. Add to the flour mixture and whisk until

1 teaspoon ground
cinnamon

1 teaspoon ground cloves

½ teaspoon baking
powder

One 15-ounce can
(1¾ cups) solid-pack
pumpkin

1 cup vegetable oil

4 large eggs

⅓ cup water

1 cup seedless raisins

combined. Do not over mix. Stir in the raisins. Transfer to the prepared pan and smooth the top.

4. Bake until the bread is golden brown and a thin wooden skewer inserted into the center comes out clean, about 55 minutes. Let cool in the pan on a wire cake rack for 15 minutes. Unmold the bread onto the rack, turn right side up, and let cool completely.

Kim's 6th birthday.

JOEY'S PECAN PIE

MAKES 8 SERVINGS

This is the best pecan pie I've ever tasted. I serve it every Thanksgiving, even though the recipe is at least four decades old. I got it from a really cute pilot named Joey who I knew way back in the day while I was working for American Airlines (before I married Robert).

A few of the girls I flew with were fabulous bakers. In the 1970s, all flight attendants were women. But Joey never gave them their due. At least not when it came to pecan pie. He always said, "I don't bake *ordinary* pecan pie, ladies; I bake make-you-cry pecan pie. Guaranteed-to-bring-home-the-blue ribbon-every-time pecan pie!"

I had my doubts, but the first time I tried Joey's recipe, I understood the meaning of the old saying, "If it's true, it's not bragging." Fair warning: Joey's recipe is as rich as it is delicious. It's not home-fries-cooked-in-grease rich. But don't-even-try-to-get-into-your-skinny-jeans-on-the-next-day rich, for sure.

This pecan pie is much less sweet than most, and dark corn syrup really gives it a richer filling. You can really taste the bourbon, which helps balance what sweetness remains, and toasted pecans gives them a bit more crunch and nutty flavor. The pie crust is a keeper, too, made with butter and moistened with egg. So, cut a slice, top it with some vanilla ice cream, and dig in.

Be sure to let the pie cool completely before serving. This is not a pie that you serve warm. In fact, it can be served chilled.

If your market sells pecan pieces, use them instead of pecan halves because it saves the mess of chopping. The pecan pieces will toast in 8 to 10 minutes.

If you don't have dark corn syrup, substitute ¾ cup plus 2 tablespoons light corn syrup with 2 tablespoons molasses (not blackstrap).

Use chopped pecans. Pies with whole pecans, painstakingly arranged on the filling in concentric circles, look pretty, but they are impossible to slice.

PIE DOUGH

1¼ cups all-purpose flour, plus more for rolling out the dough

2 teaspoons granulated sugar

¼ teaspoon salt

½ cup (1 stick) cold unsalted butter, cut into ½-inch cubes

1 large egg, beaten

1 tablespoon ice water

FILLING

1 cup dark corn syrup

⅓ cup packed light brown sugar

5 tablespoons (½ stick plus 1 tablespoon) unsalted butter, melted and slightly cooled

2 tablespoons bourbon

1 teaspoon vanilla extract

½ teaspoon salt

3 large eggs, at room temperature

1. To make the pie dough in a food processor: Pulse the flour, granulated sugar, and salt once or twice to combine them. Add the butter and pulse about six times until the mixture looks like coarse crumbs with some pea-size pieces of butter. Open the processor lid and pour the beaten egg and water over the flour mixture. Pulse about four times, just until the mixture is moistened, but do not allow it to form a ball. Press the crumbs together—they should hold together in a moist, malleable dough. If the dough is too dry, sprinkle the water over the mixture and pulse twice to combine. Remove the blade, gather up the dough, and shape it into a thick disk.

   To make the pie dough by hand: Whisk the flour, sugar, and salt together in a medium bowl to combine. Add the butter and cut in with a pastry blender or two knives until the mixture looks like coarse crumbs with some pea-size pieces of butter. Mix the egg and water together. Gradually stir in enough of the water mixture to make a moist and malleable dough. If the dough is too dry, sprinkle the water over the mixture and mix to combine. Gather up the dough and shape it into a thick disk.

2. Wrap the dough in plastic wrap. Refrigerate until chilled, at least 2 hours and up to 1 day. If the dough is cold and hard,

2 cups toasted and coarsely chopped pecan halves (see Note)

Whipped cream (page 167) or vanilla ice cream, for serving

let it stand at room temperature for 10 to 15 minutes before rolling out.

3. Unwrap the dough. Place it on a lightly floured work surface and sprinkle more flour over the top. Roll out the dough into a 12- to 13-inch round. Fit into a 9-inch pie pan, being sure the dough fits into the corners of the pan without stretching it. Trim the excess dough to a half inch overhang. Fold the dough under itself so the edge of the fold is at the edge of the pie pan and flute the dough. Prick the dough all over with a fork. Cover loosely with plastic wrap and freeze for 15 to 30 minutes.

4. Position a rack in the bottom third of the oven and preheat the oven to 400°F.

5. To make the filling: Whisk the corn syrup, brown sugar, melted butter, bourbon, vanilla, and salt together to combine. Whisk in the eggs, 1 at a time. Spread the chopped pecans in the pie crust. Pour in the filling; the pecans will float to the top.

6. Reduce the oven temperature to 350°F. Place the pie on a baking sheet and bake until the filling is evenly puffed, about 40 minutes. Let cool for 10 minutes. Transfer to a wire cooling rack and let cool completely.

7. Slice and serve with whipped cream or ice cream.

Note: To toast pecans, preheat the oven to 350°F. Spread the pecans on a large rimmed baking sheet. Bake, stirring occasionally, until toasted and fragrant, 10 to 12 minutes. Let cool before chopping.

BOOZY BUTTERSCOTCH PUDDINGS
WITH SALTED CARAMEL

MAKES 4 SERVINGS

I fell in love with a butterscotch/caramel dessert at a local restaurant near my home. So I created my own.

This butterscotch pudding is a little fancier, with caramel sauce and crunchy toffee peanuts to make a parfait. Cooks can use store-bought caramel sauce, but it's good to learn how to make it because it's an easy and quick way to add a touch of class to numerous desserts.

This is a good make-ahead dessert—add the final toppings just before serving.

Try just a touch of booze to punch up the flavor . . . or leave it out, if you wish.

PUDDING

2½ cups whole milk

½ cup heavy cream

⅓ cup cornstarch

6 large egg yolks

5 tablespoons (½ stick plus 1 tablespoon) unsalted butter

1¼ cups packed dark brown sugar

1 tablespoon bourbon or dark rum (optional)

1 teaspoon vanilla extract

1. To make the pudding: Combine the milk and heavy cream in a quart liquid measuring cup or a mixing bowl with a spout. Pour half of the milk mixture into a medium bowl. Sprinkle the cornstarch on top and whisk to dissolve it. Add the egg yolks and whisk well. Whisk in the remaining milk mixture.

2. Heat the butter in a medium heavy-bottomed saucepan over medium heat until the butter has melted and the specks at the bottom of the saucepan are light brown, about 3 minutes. Add the brown sugar and stir well until the sugar is completely moistened. Remove from the heat. Gradually

CARAMEL SAUCE

⅔ cup granulated sugar

¼ teaspoon kosher salt

½ teaspoon vanilla extract

2 tablespoons water

⅔ cup heavy cream, heated to steaming

1 tablespoon unsalted butter

WHIPPED CREAM

⅔ cup heavy cream

1½ tablespoons confectioners' sugar

½ teaspoon vanilla extract

TOPPING

⅓ cup coarsely chopped honey-roasted or toffee peanuts

whisk in the milk mixture. Return to medium heat and bring to a boil, whisking constantly and making sure to dissolve any hardened brown sugar. Reduce the heat to medium-low and let the pudding bubble, whisking often, for 1 minute. (This fully cooks the pudding; if undercooked, it will thin out after chilling.) Remove from the heat and whisk in the bourbon, if using, and vanilla.

3. Strain the pudding through a wire sieve into a medium bowl. Divide the pudding evenly among 4 dessert bowls or ramekins. Press a piece of plastic wrap directly on the surface of each pudding to cover it. Using the tip of a small knife, pierce slits in the plastic wrap to let steam escape. Refrigerate until chilled, at least 4 hours, and up to 2 days.

4. To make the caramel sauce: Stir the granulated sugar, salt, vanilla, and water in a medium saucepan over high heat until the mixture comes to a boil. Stop stirring and let the syrup boil, occasionally swirling the saucepan by the handle to combine the dark and clear areas of the syrup, until the syrup caramelizes to the color of an old penny and is lightly smoking, about 5 minutes. Remove from the heat. Carefully pour in the hot cream (the mixture will boil up) and add the butter. Return to medium heat and cook, stirring constantly, until the mixture comes to a simmer and all of the caramel has dissolved. Let cool until tepid, about 1 hour. (The sauce can be cooled, covered, and refrigerated for up to 2 days. Let come to room temperature before using.)

5. To make the whipped cream: Whip the cream, confectioners' sugar, and vanilla together in a medium bowl with an electric mixer on high speed until it forms soft peaks.

6. To serve, top each pudding with a dollop of whipped cream, a generous drizzle of sauce, and a sprinkle of peanuts. Serve chilled.

CHOCOLATE-DIPPED
COCONUT MACAROONS

MAKES 4 DOZEN

This combination of three dairy products gives these cookies a moist and chewy texture that is totally addictive. You can leave them undipped, but chocolate is a great way of gilding the lily, especially if you are making them for a holiday cookie platter. Be sure to use some kind of nonstick liner, such as baking parchment paper, on the baking sheets to keep the macaroons from sticking.

MACAROONS

One 14-ounce can sweetened condensed milk

2 tablespoons sour cream

1 tablespoon heavy cream

1½ teaspoons vanilla extract

Two 14-ounce bags sweetened flaked coconut

3 large egg whites, at room temperature

1. Position racks in the top third and center of the oven and preheat the oven to 325°F. Line two large baking sheets with parchment paper, silicone baking mats, or aluminum foil.

2. To make the cookies: In a large bowl, whisk together the condensed milk, sour cream, heavy cream, and vanilla. Add the coconut and mix until the coconut is thoroughly incorporated.

3. In a medium bowl, with an electric mixer on high speed, whip the egg whites until they form stiff, but not dry, peaks. Fold the egg whites into the coconut mixture.

4. Using a tablespoon for each macaroon, gently press and shape the coconut mixture into mounds and place about a

14 ounces bittersweet or semisweet chocolate, finely chopped

half inch apart on the baking sheets. If the cookies aren't cohesive, they could fall apart during dipping.

5. Bake until the macaroons are tinged golden brown and release easily when lifted from the baking sheet (the bottoms should be golden brown, too), about 20 minutes. Switch the positions of the baking sheets on the racks from top to bottom and front to back halfway through baking,

6. Let cool for 5 to 10 minutes on the baking sheets (if you try to lift the cookies from the sheets too soon they will fall apart). Transfer the macaroons to wire cooling racks and cool completely.

7. Repeat steps 4, 5, and 6 with any remaining dough.

8. Bring a skillet half-full of water to a bare simmer over low heat. Put the chocolate in a heatproof bowl, and place the bowl in the skillet. Be careful not to splash water into the chocolate. Using a rubber spatula, stir the chocolate often until it is smooth and melted. Remove the heatproof bowl from the water and stir constantly until the chocolate is completely melted.

9. Line two baking sheets with parchment or waxed paper. Place the bowl in a pan of warm (not hot) water to keep the chocolate fluid. One at a time, dip the macaroons in the chocolate to coat half of each cookie. Transfer to the baking sheet. Refrigerate until the chocolate is set and the macaroons release easily from the parchment, about 20 minutes. Store in an airtight container at room temperature for up to 5 days.

CHOCOLATE CHIP BANANA BREAD

MAKES 8 SERVINGS

Use very ripe (lots of brown spots) bananas, but not black and squishy. You can freeze bananas in their peels. The skin will turn black, but the flesh will be fine for baking.

Softened butter for the pan

2 cups all-purpose flour, plus more for dusting

1 teaspoon baking powder

1 teaspoon baking soda

1 teaspoon ground cinnamon

1 teaspoon salt

½ cup (1 stick) unsalted butter, at room temperature

1 cup sugar

2 large eggs, at room temperature

3 ripe bananas (1 cup), peeled and mashed

1. Position a rack in the center of the oven and preheat the oven to 350°F. Lightly butter and flour a 9 × 5 × 3-inch loaf pan, tapping out the excess flour.

2. In a medium bowl, combine the flour, baking powder, baking soda, cinnamon, and salt.

3. In a medium mixing bowl, with an electric mixer on high speed, beat the butter until smooth, about 30 seconds. Gradually add the sugar and continue beating until the mixture is pale and light in texture, about 2½ minutes more. Add the eggs, 1 at a time, beating well after each addition. In thirds, beat in the bananas. The mixture may curdle. With the mixer on low speed, in thirds, mix in the flour mixture, scraping down the sides of the bowl with a rubber spatula as needed. Do not over mix. Using a rubber spatula, fold in the

1 cup (6 ounces)
semisweet chocolate
chips

1 cup (4 ounces) coarsely
chopped pecans

chocolate chips and pecans. Transfer to the prepared pan
and smooth the top.

4. Bake until the bread is golden brown and a thin wooden
skewer inserted into the center comes out clean, about
55 minutes. Let cool in the pan on a wire cake rack for
15 minutes.

5. Unmold the bread onto the rack, turn right side up, and let
cool completely.

ACKNOWLEDGMENTS

I would like to thank all of my amazing family and lifelong friends for the incredible recipes they have shared with me throughout the years. Not only have these created some of the most magical memories in my life, they have provided some absolutely unforgettable, beautiful moments that I will treasure forever. It is my utmost honor and pleasure to be able to share these recipes with you in the hope that they will bring as much joy to your family and your loved ones as it has me and mine over the years. I truly believe that the kitchen is the heart of the home. It is the beginning and ending of each day (and sometimes the middle of the night). Have fun making your own memories and bon appétit!!!

Thank you to Charles Suitt and Karen Hunter for bringing me this cookbook project and for believing in me, and to the entire team at Simon & Schuster for your support.

My heartfelt thanks to my amazing team: Elizabeth Killmond-Roman, Jennifer

Stith, Katherine Ellena, Matthew Ryan, Karen Johnson, Todd Wilson, Joyce Bonelli, Clyde Haygood, Nick Saglimbeni, and Joyce Park. I don't know how I could ever do what I do without you guys. It takes a village! I want to thank Laura Randolph Lancaster for her extraordinary talent, diligence, and professionalism.

I want to thank my mom, Mary Jo Shannon, for raising me in such a loving home and for teaching me how to be a domestic goddess. I would like to thank Bruce Jenner for having the most voracious appetite and absolutely loving each and every recipe I ever made for you. If you didn't like it, you said you did anyway so you wouldn't hurt my feelings. For that I will always be grateful. You are the most patient man I know! Thank you to all my girlfriends, especially Lisa Miles and my cousin, CiCi Bussey, for being in my life for decades, for inspiring me in the kitchen and encouraging me to always try something new.

And for those whom I love so much but who are up in heaven: Robert Kardashian; Helen Kardashian (Nana); my grandmother, Lou Fairbanks; my dad, Harry Shannon; Auntie Dorothy; Uncle Jack; and Nicole Brown Simpson. Thank you for these amazing and beautiful recipes that remind me so much of you each and every time I create them.

I would like to thank the following companies for creating such beautiful tableware:

Hermès (pp. 6–7, 28, 80, and 134)
Christofle (pp. 6–7)
Ralph Lauren (pp. 6–7, 90, and 134)
VIETRI (pp. 41, 44, 65, 107, 110, and 122)
The Ivy on Robertson dishware (p. 53)
MacKenzie-Childs (pp. 59, 122, and 164)
Le Creuset (p. 95)

INDEX

Page numbers in *italics* refer to illustrations.

A

Aïoli, Beef Sliders with, 35–36, *37*

Aïoli, Seared Sesame Tuna with Wasabi, 89, *90*, 91

Almonds, 64, 148
   Chicken Salad with Pineapple, 63–64, *65*
   Nana's "Wedding" Rice Pilaf, *146*, 147–48

Anchovy, 55
   Grilled Shrimp Caesar Salad, 55–57
   Italian Green Salsa, 39

Anchovy Paste, 39, 66

Appetizers and dips, 17–42
   Baked Brie with Apricot Preserves, 24–25
   Beef Sliders with Aïoli, 35–36, *37*
   Bruschetta with Tomato and Basil Topping, 22–23
   CiCi's Cheese Borags, *26*, 27, *28*, 29–30
   Green Olive Tapenade, 33–34
   Italian Green Salsa, 39

   Kris's Spicy Tomato Salsa, 38
   Layered Guacamole, 40, *41*, 42
   Nicole's Chicken Nachos, *18*, 19–20, *21*
   Pâte Maîson, 31–32

Apricot Preserves, Baked Brie with, 24–25

Armenia, 15, 147, 148

Armenian Lamb Shish Kebabs, *86*, 87–88

Armenian String Beans, Auntie Dorothy's, 142

Artichoke, 123
    Pappardelle with Spring
        Vegetables, 124–25
Asparagus:
    Pan-Roasted Salmon
        with Asparagus and
        Green Olive Tapenade,
        103–4
    Pappardelle with Spring
        Vegetables, 124–25
Auntie Dorothy's Armenian
    String Beans, 142
Avocado:
    Iceberg Wedges with
        Avocado Green Goddess
        Dressing, 66–68
    Layered Guacamole, 40,
        41, 42
Azoff, Shelli, 162

B
Baked Brie with Apricot
    Preserves, 24–25
Baked goods. *See* Desserts
    and baked goods
Banana Bread, Chocolate
    Chip, 190–91
Barley, 51
    Hearty Chicken Soup,
        51–52, *53*
Bars, Magic Cookie, 170–71
Basics, 11–16
Basil, 121
    Bruschetta with Tomato
        and Basil Topping,
        22–23
    Fusilli with Tomato Basil
        Sauce, *120*, 121–22

Iceberg Wedges with
    Avocado Green Goddess
    Dressing, 66–68
Italian Green Salsa, 39
Beans, 100
    Auntie Dorothy's
        Armenian String Beans,
        142
    Black Bean and Roasted
        Corn Chicken
        Quesadillas, 99–100
    Rainbow Turkey and Bean
        Chili, 101–2
Béchamel Sauce, 118–20
Beef:
    Beef Sliders with Aïoli,
        35–36, *37*
    Bruce's Meatloaf and
        Mashies, 79, *80*, 81
    Red-and-White Lasagna,
        118–20
    Shepherd's Pie–Stuffed
        Potatoes, 92–93
    Spaghetti with Herbed
        Meatballs, 137–38
Beef Sliders with Aïoli,
    35–36, *37*
Beeshee, 4
Bell peppers:
    Armenian Lamb Shish
        Kebabs, *86*, 87–88
    Fettuccine with Sausage
        and Peppers, 115–16,
        116
    Kris's Pasta Primavera, *110*,
        111–12
    Rainbow Turkey and Bean
        Chili, 101–2

Berries, 168
    Berry Cobbler, *176*, 177–78
    Berry Crumble, 168–69
Berry Cobbler, *176*, 177–78
Berry Crumble, 168–69
Besciamella, 118
Black Bean and Roasted Corn
    Chicken Quesadillas,
    99–100
Black beans, 100
    Black Bean and Roasted
        Corn Chicken
        Quesadillas, 99–100
    Rainbow Turkey and Bean
        Chili, 101–2
Blackberries:
    Berry Cobbler, *176*,
        177–78
    Berry Crumble, 168–69
Black-eyed peas, 45
    Chicken Pot Pies, 75–77
    M.J.'s Black-Eyed Peas
        Soup, *44*, 45–46
Blueberries:
    Berry Cobbler, *176*,
        177–78
    Berry Crumble, 168–69
Boozy Butterscotch Puddings
    with Salted Caramel,
    185–87
Borags, CiCi's Cheese, *26*, 27,
    28, 29–30
Bouillon, 121
Bourbon, 182
    Boozy Butterscotch
        Puddings with Salted
        Caramel, 185–87
    Joey's Pecan Pie, 182–84

Bread:
  Bruschetta with Tomato
    and Basil Topping,
    22–23
  Chocolate Chip Banana
    Bread, 190–91
  croutons, 55
  crumbs, 137
  French, 51
  Grilled Shrimp Caesar
    Salad, 55–57
  Herbed Garlic Bread,
    160
  Herbed Sourdough Bread,
    162
  Kim's Pumpkin Bread,
    179–80
  Quick Cheese Rolls, 161
  Wild Mushroom Stuffing,
    152–54
Brie with Apricot Preserves,
  Baked, 24–25
Broccoli:
  Hearty Chicken Soup,
    51–52, 53
  Kris's Pasta Primavera, 110,
    111–12
Brown Simpson, Nicole, 19,
  21
Brownies, 172, 173–75
  Food Processor, 174–75
Bruce's Meatloaf and
  Mashies, 79, 80, 81
Bruschetta with Tomato and
  Basil Topping, 22–23
Brussels Sprouts, Roasted,
  143
Bussey, CiCi, 27

Butter, 15, 130
  Clarified Butter, 15–16
  Rich and Simple Tomato
    Sauce, 131–32
  Roast Chicken with Truffle
    Butter, 97–98
  Wild Mushroom Risotto,
    132, 133–35
Buttermilk Fried Chicken,
  Khloé's, 84–85
Butternut Squash Soup,
  Roasted, 47–48
Butterscotch Puddings with
  Salted Caramel, Boozy,
  185–87

C
Caesar Salad, Grilled Shrimp,
  55–57
Caramel, Boozy Butterscotch
  Puddings with Salted,
  185–87
Cauliflower:
  Hearty Chicken Soup,
    51–52, 53
  Truffled Cauliflower Mash,
    144–45
Cheese:
  Baked Brie with Apricot
    Preserves, 24–25
  Black Bean and Roasted
    Corn Chicken
    Quesadillas, 99–100
  CiCi's Cheese Borags, 26,
    27, 28, 29–30
  Crème Spinach Pie, 156–57
  Holiday Chopped Salad,
    58, 59, 60

Kim's Super Cheesy
    Macaroni and Cheese,
    113–14
  Lisa's Famous Mostaccioli,
    126, 127, 128
  Nicole's Chicken Nachos,
    18, 19–20, 21
  Pan-Roasted Salmon with
    Asparagus and Green
    Olive Tapenade,
    103–4
  Quick Cheese Rolls,
    161
  Red-and-White Lasagna,
    118–20
  Spaghetti with Herbed
    Meatballs, 137–38
  Turkey and Cheese
    Enchiladas, 94, 95, 96
  Wild Mushroom Risotto,
    132, 133–35
Cheesy Macaroni and
  Cheese, Kim's Super,
  113–14
Chicken:
  Black Bean and Roasted
    Corn Chicken
    Quesadillas, 99–100
  Chicken Pot Pies,
    75–77
  Chicken Salad with
    Pineapple, 63–64, 65
  Hearty Chicken Soup,
    51–52, 53
  Khloé's Buttermilk Fried
    Chicken, 84–85
  Nicole's Chicken Nachos,
    18, 19–20, 21

Chicken (*cont.*)
Pâté Maîson, 31–32
Roast Chicken with Truffle
Butter, 97–98
rotisserie, 51, 63, 94
Chicken Pot Pies, 75–77
Chicken Salad with
Pineapple, 63–64, *65*
Chiffon Pie, Lemon, *164*,
165–67
Chili, 101
Rainbow Turkey and Bean
Chili, 101–2
Thousand Island Dressing,
61–62
Chipotle, 101
Rainbow Turkey and Bean
Chili, 101–2
Chocolate:
Brownies, *172*, 173–75
Chocolate Chip Banana
Bread, 190–91
Chocolate-Dipped Coconut
Macaroons, 188–89
Magic Cookie Bars,
170–71
Chocolate Chip Banana
Bread, 190–91
Chocolate-Dipped Coconut
Macaroons, 188–89
Chopped Salad, Holiday, 58,
59, 60
Christmas, 1, 4, 7, 45, 179
CiCi's Cheese Borags, *26*, 27,
28, 29–30
Clarified Butter, 15–16
Cobbler, Berry, *176*,
177–78

Coconut:
Chocolate-Dipped Coconut
Macaroons, 188–89
Magic Cookie Bars,
170–71
Cojita, 99, 100
Black Bean and Roasted
Corn Chicken
Quesadillas, 99–100
Comfort food, 11–16
Clarified Butter, 15–16
Robert Kardashian's Cream
of Wheat, 14
Cookie Bars, Magic, 170–71
Cooking Channel, 38
Corn, 100
Black Bean and Roasted
Corn Chicken
Quesadillas, 99–100
Couscous, 103
Cranberries, 158
Cranberry Orange
Relish with Maple Syrup
and Grand Marnier,
158–59
Cranberry Orange Relish
with Maple Syrup
and Grand Marnier,
158–59
Cream, 49
Curried Pumpkin Soup, 54
Homemade Cream of
Tomato Soup, 49–50
Cream of Tomato Soup,
Homemade, 49–50
Cream of Wheat, Robert
Kardashian's, 14
Crème Spinach Pie, 156–57

Croutons, 55
Grilled Shrimp Caesar
Salad, 55–57
Crumble, Berry, 168–69
Curried Pumpkin Soup, 54
Curry:
Chicken Salad with
Pineapple, 63–64, *65*
Curried Pumpkin
Soup, 54

D
Desserts and baked goods,
163–91
Berry Cobbler, *176*,
177–78
Berry Crumble, 168–69
Boozy Butterscotch
Puddings with Salted
Caramel, 185–87
Brownies, *172*, 173–75
Chocolate Chip Banana
Bread, 190–91
Chocolate-Dipped
Coconut Macaroons,
188–89
Joey's Pecan Pie, 182–84
Kim's Pumpkin Bread,
179–80
Lemon Chiffon Pie, *164*,
165–67
Magic Cookie Bars,
170–71
Dips. *See* Appetizers
and dips
Disick, Mason, 70
Disick, Penelope, 70
DiSpirito, Rocco, 23

E

Easter, 4

Egg:

Grilled Shrimp Caesar
Salad, 55–57

Thousand Island Dressing,
61–62

Eggplant, 149

Grilled Eggplant with
Scallions and Garlic, 149,
150, 151

Enchiladas, Turkey and
Cheese, 94, *95*, 96

F

Fava beans, 123

Pappardelle with Spring
Vegetables, 124–25

Ferrare, Cristina, 51

Fettuccine with Sausage and
Peppers, 115–16, *116*

Fish. *See* Seafood

Food Processor Brownies,
174–75

Fourth of July, 4

France, 2

Fried Chicken, Khloé's
Buttermilk, 84–85

Fries, Spicy Sweet Potato
Steak, 155

Fruit:

Baked Brie with Apricot
Preserves, 24–25

Berry Cobbler, *176*,
177–78

Berry Crumble, 168–69

Chicken Salad with
Pineapple, 63–64, *65*

Chocolate Chip Banana
Bread, 190–91

Cranberry Orange Relish
with Maple Syrup and
Grand Marnier, 158–59

Holiday Chopped Salad,
58, *59*, 60

Lemon Chiffon Pie, *164*,
165–67

See also specific fruits

Fusilli with Tomato Basil
Sauce, *120*, 121–22

G

Garlic, 160

Grilled Eggplant with
Scallion and Garlic, 149,
150, 151

Herbed Garlic Bread, 160

Garvey, Candace, 79

Garvey, Steve, 79

Goat cheese, 103

Pan-Roasted Salmon with
Asparagus and Green
Olive Tapenade, 103–4

Graham crackers, 165

Graham cracker crust,
165–67

Magic Cookie Bars,
170–71

Grand Marnier, Cranberry
Orange Relish with
Maple Syrup and,
158–59

Green Beans, Auntie
Dorothy's Armenian,
142

Green Goddess, The (play), 66

Green Goddess Dressing,
Iceberg Wedges with,
66–68

Green Olive Tapenade,
33–34

Green Olive Tapenade, Pan-
Roasted Salmon with
Asparagus and, 103–4

Green Salsa, Italian, 39

Grilled Eggplant with
Scallions and Garlic, 149,
150, 151

Grilled Shrimp Caesar Salad,
55–57

Grilled Swordfish Steaks
with Tomato Salsa,
105–6, *107*

Grilled Veal Chops with
Rosemary Spice Rub,
82–83

Guacamole, Layered, 40, *41*,
42

H

Halloween, 8, 179

Hearty Chicken Soup, 51–52,
53

Herbed Garlic Bread, 160

Herbed Meatballs, Spaghetti
with, 137–38

Herbed Sourdough Bread,
162

Hermès china, 7

Holiday Chopped Salad, 58,
59, 60

Homemade Cream of Tomato
Soup 49–50

How to Live to 100, 38

I

Iceberg Wedges with Avocado Green Goddess Dressing, 66–68
Italian Green Salsa, 39
Italy, 118

J

Jalapeños, 101
  Rainbow Turkey and Bean Chili, 101–2
Jenner, Bruce, 51, *78*, 79
Jenner, Kendall, 4, 51, *67*
Jenner, Kris, *14, 21, 67, 78, 192*
Jenner, Kylie, 51, *67*
J-Lo. *See* Lopez, Jennifer
Joey's Pecan Pie, 182–84

K

Kardashian, Helen, 4, *9*, 87, 147, 148
Kardashian, Khloé, 4, *67*, 70, 84, 111, 148, 170, *181*
Kardashian, Kim, *3*, 8, 11, *12*, 13, *67*, 113, 148, 170, 179, *181*
Kardashian, Kourtney, *3*, 4, *67*, 148, 170, *181*
Kardashian, Papa, *9*
Kardashian, Rob, 8, *9*, 51, 148, 170, 173
Kardashian, Robert, 1, 2, *9*, 11, *12*, 13, 27, 87, 111, 147, 165, 182
Kebabs, Armenian Lamb Shish, *86*, 87–88
Khloé's Buttermilk Fried Chicken, 84–85

Kim's Pumpkin Bread, 179–80
Kim's Super Cheesy Macaroni and Cheese, 113–14
Kitchen, 69–71, *72*
  refrigerators, 70, *71*
  renovation, 69–70
  stove, 69–70, *72*
Kolker, Samantha, 156
Kolker, Sheila, 156
Kris's Pasta Primavera, *110*, 111–12
Kris's Spicy Tomato Salsa, 38

L

La Cornue stove, 69–70, *72*
Lamb Shish Kebabs, Armenian, *86*, 87–88
Lasagna, Red-and-White, 118–20
Layered Guacamole, 40, *41*, 42
Leeks, 144
  Chicken Pot Pies, 76
  Truffled Cauliflower Mash, 144–45
  Wild Mushroom Stuffing, 152–54
Lemon, 165
  Lemon Chiffon Pie, *164*, 165–67
Lemon Chiffon Pie, *164*, 165–67
Lettuce:
  Chicken Salad with Pineapple, 63–64, *65*

Holiday Chopped Salad, 58, *59*, 60
Iceberg Wedges with Avocado Green Goddess Dressing, 66–68
Romaine Hearts with Thousand Island Dressing, 61–62
Lisa's Famous Mostaccioli, 126, *127*, 128
Liver, 31
  Pâté Maîson, 31–32
Lopez, Jennifer, 69
Lycopene, 38

M

M.J.'s Black-Eyed Peas Soup, *44*, 45–46
Macaroni and Cheese, Kim's Super Cheesy, 113–14
Macaroons, Chocolate-Dipped Coconut, 188–89
Magic Cookie Bars, 170–71
Main courses, 73–107
  Armenian Lamb Shish Kabobs, *86*, 87–88
  Black Bean and Roasted Corn Chicken Quesadillas, 99–100
  Bruce's Meatloaf and Mashies, 79, *80*, 81
  Chicken Pot Pies, 75–77
  Grilled Swordfish Steaks with Tomato Salsa, 105–6, *107*

Grilled Veal Chops with
Rosemary Spice Rub,
82–83
Khloé's Buttermilk Fried
Chicken, 84–85
Pan-Roasted Salmon
with Asparagus and
Green Olive Tapenade,
103–4
Rainbow Turkey and Bean
Chili, 101–2
Roast Chicken with Truffle
Butter, 97–98
Seared Sesame Tuna
with Wasabi Aïoli, 89,
90, 91
Shepherd's Pie-Stuffed
Potatoes, 92–93
Turkey and Cheese
Enchiladas, 94, *95*, 96
Maple syrup, 48, 158
Cranberry Orange Relish
with Maple Syrup
and Grand Marnier,
158–59
Grade B, 48, 158
Roasted Butternut Squash
Soup, 48–49
Marinade:
Armenian Lamb Shish
Kebab, *86*, 87–88
Seared Sesame Tuna
with Wasabi Aïoli, 89,
90, 91
Mash, Truffled Cauliflower,
144–45
Mashies, Bruce's Meatloaf
and, 79, *80*, 81

Mayonnaise:
Beef Sliders with Aïoli,
35–36, *37*
Chicken Salad with
Pineapple, dressing, 63,
64
Mayonnaise Caesar Salad
Dressing, 57
Seared Sesame Tuna with
Wasabi Aïoli, 89, *90*, 91
Thousand Island Dressing,
61–62
Mayonnaise Caesar Salad
Dressing, 57
Meat:
Armenian Lamb Shish
Kebabs, *86*, 87–88
Beef Sliders with Aïoli,
35–36, *37*
Bruce's Favorite Meatloaf,
79, *80*, 81
Chicken Pot Pies, 75–77
Chicken Salad with
Pineapple, 63–64, *65*
Fettuccine with Sausage
and Peppers, 115–16,
116
Grilled Veal Chops with
Rosemary Spice Rub,
82–83
Hearty Chicken Soup,
51–52, *53*
Khloé's Buttermilk Fried
Chicken, 84–85
Lisa's Famous Mostaccioli,
126, *127*, 128
Nicole's Chicken Nachos,
18, 19–20, *21*

Pâté Maîson, 31–32
Rainbow Turkey and Bean
Chili, 101–2
Red-and-White Lasagna,
118–20
Roast Chicken with Truffle
Butter, 97–98
Shepherd's Pie-Stuffed
Potatoes, 92–93
Spaghetti with Herbed
Meatballs, 137–38
Turkey and Cheese
Enchiladas, 94, *95*, 96
Meatballs, Spaghetti
with Herbed,
137–38
Meatloaf and Mashies,
Bruce's 79, *80*, 81
Medina, Debbie, *21*
Miles, Lisa, 125
Milk:
Béchamel Sauce, 118–20
Khloé's Buttermilk Fried
Chicken, 84–85
solids, 15
Mint:
Iceberg Wedges with
Avocado Green
Goddess Dressing,
66–68
Italian Green Salsa, 39
Mostaccioli, Lisa's Famous,
126, *127*, 128
Mushroom:
Wild Mushroom Risotto,
132, 133–35
Wild Mushroom Stuffing,
152–54

N

Nachos, Nicole's Chicken, *18*, 19–20, *21*

Nana's "Wedding" Rice Pilaf, *146*, 147–48

New Year's, 45

Nicole's Chicken Nachos, *18*, 19–20, *21*

Nuts:

Brownies, *172*, 173–75

Chicken Salad with Pineapple, 63–64, *65*

Chocolate Chip Banana Bread, 190–91

Holiday Chopped Salad, 58, *59*, 60

Joey's Pecan Pie, 182–84

Magic Cookie Bars, 170–71

O

Oil, 15

olive, 22

Olive, 33

Castelnuovo, 33

Green Olive Tapenade, 33–34

Layered Guacamole, 40, *41*, 42

Pan-Roasted Salmon with Asparagus and Green Olive Tapenade, 103–4

Olive oil, extra-virgin, 22

Onion:

Armenian Lamb Shish Kebabs, *86*, 87–88

Rich and Simple Tomato Sauce, 131–32

Orange Relish with Maple Syrup and Grand Marnier, Cranberry, 158–59

P

Pan-Roasted Salmon with Asparagus and Green Olive Tapenade, 103–4

Pappardelle with Spring Vegetables, 124–25

Paprika, 40, 64, 82, 85, 102, 114

Rainbow Turkey and Bean Chili, 101–2

Rosemary Spice Rub, 82

Spanish smoked sweet, 102. *See also* Pimentón de la Vera.

Paris, 31

Pasta, 109–37

Fettuccine with Sausage and Peppers, 115–16, *116*

Fusilli with Tomato Basil Sauce, *120*, 121–22

Kim's Super Cheesy Macaroni and Cheese, 113–14

Kris's Pasta Primavera, *110*, 111–12

Lisa's Famous Mostaccioli, 126, *127*, 128

Pappardelle with Spring Vegetables, 124–25

Penne with Vodka Sauce, 129–30

Red-and-White Lasagna, 118–20

Rich and Simple Tomato Sauce, 131–32

Spaghetti with Herbed Meatballs, 137–38

Wild Mushroom Risotto, *132*, 133–35

Pastry:

Baked Brie with Apricot Preserves, 24–25

Cici's Cheese Borags, *26*, 27, *28*, 29–30

Pâté Maîson, 31–32

Peas, 123

Chicken Pot Pies, 75–77

M.J. Black-Eyed Peas Soup, *44*, 45–46

Pappardelle with Spring Vegetables, 124–25

Pecans:

Chocolate Chip Banana Bread, 190–91

Holiday Chopped Salad, 58, *59*, 60

Joey's Pecan Pie, 182–84

Magic Cookie Bars, 170–71

Penne with Vodka Sauce, 129–30

Pie:

Chicken Pot Pies, 75–77

Crème Spinach Pie, 156–57

Joey's Pecan Pie, 182–84

Lemon Chiffon Pie, *164*, 165–67

Shepherd's Pie–Stuffed Potatoes, 92–93

Pilaf, Nana's "Wedding" Rice, *146*, 147–48

Pimentón de la Vera, 102. *See* Paprika.

Pineapple, Chicken Salad with, 63–64, *65*

Pine nuts, *33*

Pork:
Fettuccine with Sausage and Peppers, 115–16, *116*
M.J.'s Black-Eyed Peas Soup, *44*, 45–46
Red-and-White Lasagna, 118–20
Spaghetti with Herbed Meatballs, 137–38

Potato:
Bruce's Meatloaf and Mashies, 79, *80*, 81
Shepherd's Pie-Stuffed Potatoes, 92–93
Spicy Sweet Potato Steak Fries, 155
Sweet Potato Soufflé, *140*, 141

Pot Pies, Chicken, 75–77

Preserves, Baked Brie with Apricot, 24–25

Puddings with Salted Caramel, Boozy Butterscotch, 185–87

Pumpkin, 8
Curried Pumpkin Soup, 54
Kim's Pumpkin Bread, 179–80

Q

Quatre épices, 31

Quesadillas, Black Bean and Roasted Corn Chicken, 99–100

Quick Cheese Rolls, 161

Quinoa, 103

R

Rainbow Turkey and Bean Chili, 101–2

Raisins, 148
Nana's "Wedding" Rice Pilaf, *146*, 147–48

Raspberries:
Berry Cobbler, *176*, 177–78
Berry Crumble, 168–69

Red-and-White Lasagna, 118–20

Refrigerators, 70, *71*

Relish with Maple Syrup and Grand Marnier, Cranberry Orange, 158–59

Rice, 133
Arborio, 133
Nana's "Wedding" Rice Pilaf, *146*, 147–48
Wild Mushroom Risotto, *132*, 133–35

Rice Pilaf, Nana's "Wedding," *146*, 147–48

Rich and Simple Tomato Sauce, 131–32

Risotto, Wild Mushroom, *132*, 133–35

Roast Chicken with Truffle Butter, 97–98

Roasted Brussels Sprouts, 143

Roasted Butternut Squash Soup, 47–48

Roasted Corn Chicken Quesadillas, Black Bean and, 99–100

Roasted Salmon with Asparagus and Green Olive Tapenade, Pan, 103–4

Robert Kardashian's Cream of Wheat, 14

Rolls, Quick Cheese, 161

Romaine Hearts with Thousand Island Dressing, 61–62

Rosemary Spice Rub, Grilled Veal Chops with, 82–83

Rotisserie chicken, 51, 63, 94

Rub, Grilled Veal Chops with Rosemary Spice, 82–83

S

Salad, 43, 55–68
Chicken Salad with Pineapple, 63–64, *65*
Grilled Shrimp Caesar Salad, 55–57
Holiday Chopped Salad, 58, *59*, 60
Iceberg Wedges with Avocado Green Goddess Dressing, 66–68

Salad (*cont.*)

Romaine Hearts with
Thousand Island
Dressing, 61–62

Seared Sesame Tuna with
Wasabi Aïoli, 89, *90*, 91

Salad dressings:

Caesar, 55–57

Chicken Salad with
Pineapple, dressing for,
63

Iceberg Wedges with
Avocado Green Goddess
Dressing, 66–68

Mayonnaise Caesar Salad
Dressing, 57

Thousand Island Dressing,
61–62

Vinaigrette, 58

Salmon, 103

Pan-Roasted Salmon with
Asparagus and Green
Olive Tapenade, 103–4

Salsa:

Grilled Swordfish Steaks
with Tomato Salsa,
105–6, *107*

Italian Green Salsa, 39

Kris's Spicy Tomato Salsa,
38

Salted Caramel, Boozy
Butterscotch Puddings
with, 185–87

Sausage:

Lisa's Famous Mostaccioli,
126, *127*, 128

Red-and-White Lasagna,
118–20

Spaghetti with Herbed
Meatballs, 137–38

Sausage and Peppers,
Fettuccine with, 115–16,
116

Scallions and Garlic, Grilled
Eggplant with, 149, *150*,
151

Seafood:

Grilled Shrimp Caesar
Salad, 55–57

Grilled Swordfish Steaks
with Tomato Salsa,
105–6, *107*

Pan-Roasted Salmon
with Asparagus and
Green Olive Tapenade,
103–4

Seared Sesame Tuna
with Wasabi Aïoli, 89,
90, 91

Seared Sesame Tuna
with Wasabi Aïoli, 89,
90, 91

Sesame Tuna with Wasabi
Aïoli, Seared, 89, *90*, 91

Setting the table, 5, *6*, 7,
7, 8

Shannon, Mary Jo, 45

Shepherd's Pie–Stuffed
Potatoes, 92–93

Shish Kebabs, Armenian
Lamb, *86*, 87–88

Shrimp, 55

Grilled Shrimp Caesar
Salad, 55–57

size of, 55

Shulman, Linda, *21*

Side dishes. *See* Vegetables
and sides

Simple Tomato Sauce,
Rich and, 131–32

Sliders with Aïoli, Beef,
35–36, *37*

Soufflé, Sweet Potato, *140*, 141

Soup, 43–54

Curried Pumpkin Soup, 54

Hearty Chicken Soup,
51–52, *53*

Homemade Cream
of Tomato Soup, 49–50

M.J.'s Black-Eyed Peas
Soup, *44*, 45–46

Roasted Butternut Squash
Soup, 47–48

Sour cream, 40

Layered Guacamole, 40,
41, 42

Sourdough Bread, Herbed,
162

Spaghetti with Herbed
Meatballs, 137–38

Spice Rub, Grilled Veal Chops
with Rosemary, 82–83

Spicy Sweet Potato Steak
Fries, 155

Spicy Tomato Salsa, Kris's, 38

Spinach, 156

Crème Spinach Pie, 156–57

Spring Vegetables,
Pappardelle with, 124–25

Squash, 47

Roasted Butternut Squash
Soup, 47–48

Stoves, 69

La Cornue, 69–70, *72*

St. Patrick's Day, 8

String Beans, Auntie Dorothy's Armenian, 142

Stuffing, Wild Mushroom, 152–54

Sunday dinners, 5

Super Cheesy Macaroni and Cheese, Kim's, 113–14

Sushi, 89

Sweet Potato Soufflé, *140*, 141

Sweet Potato Steak Fries, Spicy, 155

Swordfish Steaks with Tomato Salsa, Grilled, 105–6, *107*

T

Table settings, 5, *6*, 7, *7*, 8

Tapenade:
    Green Olive Tapenade, 33–34
    Pan-Roasted Salmon with Asparagus and Green Olive Tapenade, 103–4

Thanksgiving, 2, 8, 47, 94, 141

Thousand Island Dressing, Romaine Hearts with, 61–62

Thyme, 130
    Rich and Simple Tomato Sauce, 131–32
    Roast Chicken with Truffle Butter, 97–98

Tomato:
    Armenian Lamb Shish Kebabs, *86*, 87–88

Auntie Dorothy's Armenian String Beans, 142

Bruschetta with Tomato and Basil Topping, 22–23

Fusilli with Tomato Basil Sauce, *120*, 121–22

Grilled Swordfish Steaks with Tomato Salsa, 105–6, *107*

Homemade Cream of Tomato Soup, 49–50

Kris's Spicy Tomato Salsa, 38

Layered Guacamole, 40, *41*, 42

Lisa's Famous Mostaccioli, 126, *127*, 128

Penne with Vodka Sauce, 129–30

Red-and-White Lasagna, 118–20

Rich and Simple Tomato Sauce, 131–32

Spaghetti with Herbed Meatballs, 137–38

Tone, setting the, 5–8

Trader Joe's, 48, 100

Truffle Butter, Roast Chicken, 97–98

Truffled Cauliflower Mash, 144–45

Truffle oil, 144

Tuna, 89
    Seared Sesame Tuna with Wasabi Aïoli, 89, *90*, 91

Turkey, 94, 152
    Lisa's Famous Mostaccioli, 126, *127*, 128
    Rainbow Turkey and Bean Chili, 101–2
    Turkey and Cheese Enchiladas, 94, *95*, 96
    Wild Mushroom Stuffing, 152–54

Turkey and Cheese Enchiladas, 94, *95*, 96

V

Veal Chops with Rosemary Spice Rub, Grilled, 82–83

Vegetables and sides, 139–62
    Auntie Dorothy's Armenian String Beans, 142
    Cranberry Orange Relish with Maple Syrup and Grand Marnier, 158–59
    Crème Spinach Pie, 156–57
    Grilled Eggplant with Scallions and Garlic, 149, *150*, 151
    Herbed Garlic Bread, 160
    Herbed Sourdough Bread, 162
    Nana's "Wedding" Rice Pilaf, *146*, 147–48
    Pappardelle with Spring Vegetables, 124–25
    Quick Cheese Rolls, 161

Vegetables and sides (*cont.*)
    Roasted Brussels Sprouts,
      143
    Spicy Sweet Potato Steak
      Fries, 155
    Sweet Potato Soufflé, *140,*
      141
    Truffled Cauliflower Mash,
      144–45
    Wild Mushroom Stuffing,
      152–54
    See also Salad; *specific*
      vegetables

Vienna, 2
Vinaigrette, 58
Vodka Sauce, Penne with,
    129–30

W
Walnuts:
    Brownies, *172,* 173–75
Wasabi Aïoli, Seared Sesame
    Tuna with, 89, *90,* 91
"Wedding" Rice Pilaf, Nana's,
    146, 147–48
West, North, 70

Wheat, Robert Kardashian's
    Cream of, 14
Wild Mushroom Risotto, *132,*
    133–35
Wild Mushroom Stuffing,
    152–54

Z
Zucchini:
    Hearty Chicken Soup,
      51–52, *53*
    Kris's Pasta Primavera, *110,*
      111–12

ABOUT THE AUTHOR

KRIS JENNER is an entrepreneur, a *New York Times* bestselling author, and the creator, executive producer, and star of the E! Network's award-winning reality series, *Keeping Up with the Kardashians*. She is CEO of her own production company, Jenner Communications, and she manages the careers of her six children: Kourtney, Kim, Khloé, Rob, Kendall, and Kylie.